FAST BOWLING

WITH
BOB WILLIS

FAST BOWLING

WITH
BOB WILLIS

WILLOW BOOKS
Collins
8 Grafton Street, London W1
1984

Willow Books
William Collins Sons & Co Ltd
London · Glasgow · Sydney · Auckland
Toronto · Johannesburg

British Library Cataloguing in Publication Data

Willis, Bob
Fast Bowling with Bob Willis.
1. Cricket—Bowling
I. Title
796.358'22   GV917

ISBN 0-00-218022-7

Set in Bembo
by Ace Filmsetting Ltd, Frome, Somerset
Printed and bound in Great Britain by
William Collins Sons & Co Ltd, Glasgow

All photographs by Ken Keddy apart from the following:
Patrick Eagar, pages 8, 49; Sport & General Press Agency page 15.

Contents

Preface

This book is aimed at fast bowlers of all ages and from all levels of the game. I have tried to cover all the problems a fast bowler faces, whether he is a schoolboy who has at last stopped growing, a club player whose bowling arm gets no higher as the years roll by, or a budding professional coming to terms with the rigours of first-class cricket. As a fast bowler myself, I have concentrated on that particular facet, but I have not forgotten seam or swing bowlers – indeed many of the principles expounded apply to all three styles.

I hope cricket coaches will also read this book because fast bowling needs constructive guidance as well as hard work and intelligence. To the school cricket master, the club senior pro and the county coach, I say this: think harder about bringing the best out of your fast bowlers. English cricket needs them.

For the purposes of simplicity, I have discussed the art of fast bowling as it applies to the right-hander. The fundamentals are equally relevant to the left-hander and all that is needed is obvious adjustment.

Finally I would like to thank Ken Kelly for his informative photographs and Patrick Murphy for distilling my thoughts and getting them into book form.

Bob Willis
December 1983

Victory in the air as Lawson falls to an outswinger during my best spell of bowling for England – 8 for 43 at Headingly, 1981.

1
WHAT MAKES A FAST BOWLER?

When I sit down and analyse the many ingredients that go into making a fast bowler good enough to play for his country, I wonder how I ever made it. In my case, I suppose hard work was the crucial asset I picked up, to graft on to my natural speed. Heaven knows I possess enough defects to disqualify me for the description of a coach's dream fast bowler. My run-up has been described as resembling a broken-down biplane and certainly my charging, aggressive run to the wicket owes everything to effort and little to finesse. When I get to the wicket, my action is open-chested and, as a result, it puts great strain on a physique that is not terribly impressive.

I had been in first-class cricket for ten years before I realized what a bizarre run-up and action I possessed and the discovery came courtesy of my England team-mate, Graham Gooch. Graham's impersonations of certain bowlers enlivened several Tests that were drawing to a predictable close, and the first time he impersonated me, I did not know where to look. Of course, it was funny and I could see the joke, but I thought, 'Do I really look like that when I'm bowling?' The fast bowler never gets a chance to examine his action unless he sits down with endless pictures in front of him, or commissions a video cameraman to record the whole process from start of run-up to follow through. The edited highlights on television also give little indication of the intrinsic merits of the fast bowler's art because the camera looks down the wicket and does not concentrate on the fast bowler's run-up. So when I saw Graham's jangling legs, pumping right arm and exaggerated chest-on delivery, I found myself thinking for the umpteenth time, 'How did I slip through the net? How have I managed to bowl so long for England?'

I suppose the first reason is vital – luck. Lucky with the quality of advice I have received, lucky with the skilled surgery that has saved my career on several occasions, but, above all, very fortunate that I could bowl fast naturally. Fast bowlers are born, not made. Of course, the machine can be tuned to a better pitch, the model can be slimmed down or refined, but there is no substitute for the ability to whip the arm over very quickly at the moment of releasing the ball. If you gather ten boys together in the nets and ask them to bowl as fast as possible, one of them will stand out – he will have a natural whippiness and pace that sets him apart. He may lack style, co-ordination of movement but somehow he contrives to project a cricket ball at speed to the other end of the wicket. Unless your arm is a blur at the moment of delivery, you will never make a fast bowler. You may be able to master the arts of seam and swing and deliver an occasional ball that will make the batsman hop around a bit – but forget about being a genuine quick bowler and console yourself with the thought that it is simply a matter of natural ability.

Ever since I was a boy I could somehow bowl quickly. I was taller than most of my age and at school I simply ran up and bowled as fast as possible. I went to a rugby-playing school in Guildford and endured miserable winters, trying to get the hang of the bizarre activities that went on in the scrum. I used to think to myself, 'I'll get my own back on you lot in the summer,' and would dream of scattering the stumps and frightening the batsmen. Looking back on it all now, I recall that my opening partner in the school first eleven had a magnificent, textbook bowling action – yet the ball did not travel very quickly to the other end. I was all over the place in my run-up and just hurled the ball down without much thought . . . yet I was fast.

Of course, the basic ability to be fast is not enough when you start to progress in cricket. So much else must be grafted on to that priceless asset. The greatest fast bowler of my time has been Dennis Lillee, a man with a classical action but also a deep thinker on the art of fast bowling. I once asked him what were the most important qualities needed to be a fast bowler and his answer was typically thorough. He listed ten assets in the following order of priority:

1. The ability to bowl fast
2. Stamina and physical fitness
3. 'Killer' instinct
4. The ability to 'think' a batsman out
5. The ability to swing the ball at will
6. The ability to bowl a good bouncer and yorker
7. A good captain
8. Good fielders, particularly the slips and wicketkeeper
9. A fast, bouncy wicket
10. The ability to cut the ball off the wicket

I would not take issue with much of that, although I do feel that luck should never be underestimated. Perhaps Dennis has overdone the 'killer' instinct a little too much for my liking, and as a bowler operating mainly in English conditions, I would place the ability to cut the ball off the wicket a little higher in my list. In England, we are used to bowling on green wickets and it is always important to be able to capitalise on a pitch that favours your particular bowling skills. I also feel the knack of concentration is every bit as important for a fast bowler as a batsman – you need to be able to plan an over to suit a particular stage of a game and to possess the mental strength to carry the strategy through. The fast bowler should always be thinking about the next delivery as he walks back, and able to clear 'the red mists' from his eyes if he has just been slammed to the boundary. He must also be strong-minded; he must genuinely feel that this is going to be his day, not that of any batsman. By force of will, he must strive to make the game go his way – 'I'm in charge' should be the motto of the fast bowlers' union.

He should always want to bowl, to be ready to answer the captain's call at the end of an innings when most of his colleagues are shattered and longing for the sanctuary of the dressing-room and a long, cool drink. If the fast bowler has been doing his job properly, he should be more fatigued than anyone, yet he is the one who is expected to achieve a breakthrough at any stage of the game. He must relish such responsibility. Men like Fred Trueman and Dennis Lillee were great fast bowlers for many reasons, but their inner-conviction that each delivery of theirs was about to get a wicket saw them through many gruelling sessions when lesser men would have simply gone through the motions. A fast bowler must have that extra bit of 'devil'; without wishing to see a batsman injured, he must try to keep him apprehensive. No one likes a fast delivery slamming into the ribs, or seeing a really quick one rear off a length towards the face. It is a hard, relentless game in the higher echelons and as long as the fast bowling stops short of intimidation, I see no reason why the batsman should have an easy time of it out there in the middle. There is a certain pleasure in beating the batsman by sheer speed and watching him rub the injured part of the body: unless the fast bowler relished such a moral victory, he lacks that essential fire in his belly.

I was interested to hear Dennis Lillee put stamina and physical fitness second in his list of crucial assets for a fast bowler. I fully agree – if you are fit, you are automatically a better performer. You can switch on to that reserve-tank of energy when necessary and continue attacking with the ball. If you are not gasping for oxygen after every delivery, you can maintain your concentration and work out where to bowl at the particular batsman. As I know to my cost, when fatigue starts seeping into the fast bowler's consciousness, he is there for the taking; because of the sheer speed involved, the ball goes off the bat just as quickly when direction and rhythm have gone awry. There is a dreadful feeling of humiliation involved in running 35 yards at speed, trying to deliver the ball as fast as you can and seeing it steered contemptuously away to the boundary by an arrogant batsman. Morale slumps, the fatigue seems to take an even greater toll of your resources and the initiative has passed to the batsman. We all experience that slump in our playing fortunes, but if you are fit enough, you can still win the battle. If you have shown enough resilience to stick at a regulated and sensible training programme before the start of the season, then you can call on reserves of stamina during a match. Many a game at all levels is won by hard work done in the gym or by road-running several months earlier.

I discovered the importance of training and fitness programmes rather late in my career and in embarrassing circumstances. I had played more than 20 times for England before someone pointed out to me that I just was not fit enough. Tony Greig was England captain at the time and he dispensed some home truths to me at a barbecue in Sydney. We had just lost the Centenary Test by a narrow margin and Greig told me that if I had been properly trained, England would have triumphed. At the time, I dismissed his remarks in my customary abrupt manner when a nerve-end is touched, but it got me thinking. Ian Chappell had said something similar a few years earlier – 'Willis is there for the taking after lunch, he just caves in' – but I merely thought it was a case of an aggressive Australian having a cheap jibe at my expense. I began to think there might have been some substance to his remarks after my discussion with Tony Greig. My professional pride had been stung and so I decided to work hard at my training. I became fitter, stronger, more confident and a more effective fast bowler.

So if an England fast bowler can revolutionize his attitude to physical fitness at the age of 28, so can any of you budding fast bowlers, you schoolboys or teenagers who have grown complacent at the amount of wickets you take by simply running up and bowling as fast as you can. You will become an even better bowler if you get fitter, I promise you – and the same goes to all cricketers of any age. More than any other aspect of a fast bowler's repertoire, this one is completely in the hands of the individual.

Assuming that a fast bowler attains a satisfactory standard of fitness, he may still struggle because of basic defects in his physique. Generally, I would say that an ideal fast bowler's build would be between 5ft 9ins and 6ft 4ins, with a well-proportioned and muscled body. Now I know that I hardly qualify on those counts, but let us take height first. A smallish person will be at a great disadvantage if he aspires to bowl quickly: quite simply he will lack that ability to get the ball to bounce disconcertingly. Good batsmen are troubled by deliveries that rear up sharply, not by someone bowling accurately at the stumps all the time. The higher a bowler's arm when the ball is released, the more bounce he will get from the pitch. I suppose my height (6ft 6ins) has been one of my greatest assets as a fast bowler, because if I put enough effort into my delivery, I can usually wring some bounce from slow, unresponsive wickets. It is a great feeling to make a good player adjust at the last instant because he has been surprised by a ball that rises rapidly, and an even better feeling when he cannot get out of the way of the delivery and fends it off to a close-catcher. All the hard work is justified at that moment, I can assure you.

The fast bowler should also be well co-ordinated and athletic. This is an area where I am a distinct also-ran. I am the original tall, gawky man with the graceful bearing of a camel – partly a hereditary thing, but also the legacy from operations to my knees. I console myself with the knowledge that my extra few inches of height compensates, but I do envy the loose-limbed athleticism of fast bowlers I have known during my career . . . men like John Snow, Dennis Lillee, Jeff Thomson and Michael Holding. A natural extension to their beautiful bowling actions was their athleticism in the field and I envied their ability to move swiftly to the ball in the field, to bend easily and throw elegantly. Perhaps that is why I always make a point of watching a young fast bowler fielding as well as delivering the ball: if he is supple and co-ordinated while fielding, he should be the same when running in to bowl.

Flexibility of limbs is very important to a fast bowler. He should be able to move freely in all his muscle areas while not sacrificing vital explosiveness at the moment of delivery. That explosiveness comes from the strength of the appropriate muscles and the speed at which they can contract. Now I do not wish to get too technical on this point, but unless your muscles are able to contract fast enough to withstand the physical pressure of exploding at the instant of delivery, then you cannot bowl fast and never will. At the delivery point, weak muscles in the groin and hamstring areas can easily be injured under the stress. You also need to be strong in the chest, arms and shoulders to withstand that explosiveness. In the end, suppleness – the ability to avoid twanging a hamstring at the slightest sign of stress – is more important to a fast bowler than sheer muscular strength. Cricket history is adorned with examples of great fast bowlers who were not particularly tall nor impressively built – but they had flexible muscles that enabled them to deliver a ball at great speed.

The consolation to the budding fast bowler who possesses an average physique is that he can still make it, provided he has the basic ability to bowl fast and the will to work at his training. Look no further than my own career to prove the point.

One crucial question I would put to anyone who has the basic ingredients to be an authentic quick bowler: Do you really *want* to be a fast bowler? The word 'motivation' has been grossly over-used in sporting circles in recent years, but there is no doubt in my mind that self-motivation is absolutely essential for a fast bowler. He will need it to make light of inadequate practice facilities, the lack of specialist coaching, a climate that does not favour such a demanding form of physical exercise – and, above all, he will have to rely on himself to get through the hours of training and polishing up technique in the nets. When I look at the list of qualities needed, I thank heaven I possess a fair amount of them, but I also bemoan the fact that few youngsters in England now seem to want to try to become top-class fast bowlers.

In the last 40 years, England have only produced five front-line fast bowlers – Frank Tyson, Fred Trueman, Brian Statham, John Snow and myself. In a land where cricket is played by so many people, I think that is criminal, especially as Test cricket is being dominated more and more by the fast men. They come from overseas to play in our County Championship, learn how to bowl in English conditions, then roll us over in Tests while we seem to be standing still in our development of fast bowlers. Of course, the weather does not help; invariably the season begins in foul conditions and the fast bowler is loath to let himself go in the cold in case he pulls a muscle. The climate also makes the job of a grounds-man more difficult. Ideally a fast bowler needs a hard, quick wicket of even bounce so that he will be rewarded for putting effort into his bowling. Unfortunately, such wickets are a thing of the past in England. I believe that groundsmen have in their own little way contributed to the demise of the English quick bowler by turning out lifeless, bland wickets that favour no one, or green tracks that reward the seam bowler who can move the ball a little either way and keep the batsman guessing. County committees have exerted undue pressure on groundsmen to produce wickets that favour the home teams, resulting generally in surfaces that do not help the bowler prepared to work hardest of all at his craft – the spinner and the genuine fast bowler. The art of groundsmanship in the first-class game has not kept pace with sophisticated advances on other fronts and one of the end-products of that is the decline of English fast bowlers. With so little creativity coming from county groundsmen, it is little wonder that those charged with responsibility for wickets in club and schoolboy cricket often get them wrong. Flat, slow pitches with little bounce are no good to any cricketers of genuine ability – least of all the fast bowler.

Yet having made due allowance for the poor standard of wickets, what hap-pens to the millions of youngsters who start out determined to be the next Trueman? In many cases, they have such excesses of imagination coached out of them. In England, there seems to be an obsession with 'line-and-length' bowling among the coaching fraternity; youngsters who can bowl quick are forever being told 'slow down a bit, get your line and length first'. In my opinion that is nonsense. If a lad has the ability given only to a few to run and bowl fast, then he should be encouraged to build on that priceless asset, not to jettison it in

Fred Trueman and Brian Statham, two of England's greatest fast bowlers. All young boys have their heroes and mine was Brian Statham, whose stature inspired me and made me want to become a fast bowler. If you are keen and observant enough, then you cannot fail to improve your technique by analysing those fast bowlers currently at the top of their tree.

favour of the conventional virtues of bowling straight. There is plenty of time to master the undoubted necessities of pitching the ball where you want, of bowling straight, but it is a sin and a shame to hear about youngsters who have their speed coached out of them. The cricket master at school has a responsibility to remember that height far outgrows strength among boys: he must be patient with his beanpole of an opening bowler who gets tired because he lacks stamina. He must not settle for 12 overs of medium pace instead of six wayward overs of undeniable speed. Too often, a young fast bowler opts for being competent rather than occasionally inspired and invariably his mentor is responsible for this depressing preference towards conformity. The trend towards the competent continues in the higher strata of the game, even into first-class cricket. Too many disciplined, uniform cricketers with no flair are being turned out by unimaginative coaches and the chief sufferer on this production line of mediocrity is the quick bowler.

No such conformities are acceptable in places like South Africa, Australia or the West Indies. As I know from my many tours to these countries, young fast bowlers are actively encouraged. Take the West Indies; of course the climate is ideal for fast bowling because the ball whips through the air that much faster, and also the lithe, strong physique of the West Indian is ideally suited to bowling fast. When you watch them play cricket on the beaches or in the streets, observe how those under ten throw the ball, rather than bowl it: even at that age, they are trying to be fast, so that when they grow a little taller and stronger, they automatically take a long run-up and bowl as fast as they can. There is also a fast-bowling heritage in the Caribbean. Apart from Gibbs, Ramadhin and Valentine their illustrious bowlers have all been of the 'speed-of-light' variety; the success of Constantine spawned a host of imitators all the way through to Holding. With many deprived areas in the West Indies, the ability to bowl very fast is a passport to a better way of life, to social and professional respectability. When a boy from the back streets of Kingston sees the West Indies triumph both in Tests and World Cup competitions because of a fearsome array of fast-bowling talent, he automatically identifies with the quickies; he aims for their pedestal, he wants to be one of their successors. He will be lucky in his natural ability to bowl fast, his environment that worships cricket and in the absence of sophisticated coaches with impressive qualifications who would invariably counsel caution.

The change of environment must be the main reason why hardly any British-born black fast bowlers have come through to prominence. After all, the black person's loose-limbed athletic physique is absolutely ideal for the rigours of bowling fast, and the mere fact that a boy is born in Bradford or Birmingham, as opposed to the Caribbean, does not reduce his basic ability to be a quick bowler. So why are there so few quickies among the first-generation black Englishmen? One must take account of the poor climate and the lack of adequate facilities in many schools, but above all I think they get softened up by the prevailing *laissez-faire* attitude in English society. Quite simply, bowling fast is too much like hard work for the bulk of youngsters in England. I watch them in the nets at schools and even in our Colts games at Edgbaston: too many prefer to follow the coach's advice, drop their pace and bowl there or thereabouts for a few overs and avoid working up a sweat. Not enough youngsters have the resilience to say to themselves: 'I know I can bowl fast, and I'm going to work at it.' On English wickets, you can usually get away with bowling little seamers to a defensive field; it invariably works at county level because of the deteriorating quality of wickets, so why should a youngster try extra hard to be a fast bowler when he has watched first-class cricketers opting for conformity?

I am reluctant to go on at great length with comparisons of different generations, but it does seem to me that our modern society cushions youngsters too much, so that they lack inherent toughness when they face challenges in the sporting field. They may have the latest gear bought for them by indulgent parents, or the best coaching that money can buy, but there is no substitute for hard unyielding work and the ability to stand on one's own two feet. I become more and more disenchanted as I see young first-class cricketers playing at their profession; I fully support those who want to play the game for fun and I wish them well, but so many coming into county cricket feel the game owes them a living. If you try to sharpen up their ideas about net practice or training, the reaction is invariably a passive one. There seems to be a subconscious will towards levelling off the standards, as if it is the wrong thing to be too determined about making it to the top through self-motivation and pride in performance. This mood of complacency among modern cricket's youngsters is, of course, totally harmful to the budding fast bowler. It is so easy to get sucked into the morass of mediocrity, where you can get by without aiming really high. In this respect, strength of character is almost as important as natural ability to the young quickie. He must grit his teeth, tell himself he wants to improve, that he can always go out and have a few pints some other evening, that he should be out pounding through the park in his tracksuit rather than lying in bed reading a newspaper.

How can I convince youngsters and club cricketers about the joys of finally making it to the top by dint of sheer hard work? If I say that nothing in life is easy, that sweat and tears must be spilt to achieve anything worthwhile – well, that would probably be just passed over as preaching. I shall try another argument: fast bowlers win matches at any level of the game. Captains base their strategy round the availability of the new ball and those who have the appropriate firepower have no qualms about hammering away at the batsmen with a battery of fast bowlers. Nobody likes batting against the quicks at any level: it is a dangerous, instinctive business demanding nerve, bravery and a clear eye. Recent electronic tests have revealed that a fast bowler who manages to reach a delivery speed of 90 mph gives the batsman about 0.6 seconds to play the ball – half of that involves sighting the ball and deciding what to do about it, and the other 0.3 seconds is taken up with performing the stroke. One can obviously symphathize with the batsman in such circumstances, but these figures only underline the importance of a fast bowler. If he manages to get all his component parts in full working order – speed, control, variety, the element of surprise – then he can be devastating, a matchwinner. In my own humble way, I have managed to scale those heights on occasions and I can assure you the rare peaks are worth the troughs one invariably experiences. You are in control of the game, the batsman is at your mercy and the crowd relish the excitement of a fast bowler at the top of his form. It is pure theatre, a gladiatorial atmosphere as the batsman nervously awaits the sprinting athlete with the ball in his hand. The roaring crowd urging on the bowler, the collective intake of breath as he delivers, then – whoosh! – the blur of the ball and the smack into the wicketkeeper's gloves a second later. When you know that your controlled speed and technical ability are going to be decisive, when you sense that this is, after all, going to be your day – that is a marvellous feeling. Cricket may be a team game, but there remains the individual contest between bat and ball. Bowler and batsman are isolated and whoever triumphs helps to win the wider contest. Your captain is relying on you, he gives you the field you want, your best fielders are in the catching positions. It now all depends on you, the fast bowler. Are you up to the responsibility? No one ever knows until battle is joined, but for anyone who wants to be more than just a bit-player on the cricketing stage, it is a moment to savour.

I believe the fast bowler can be the most influential person in a cricket match if he can rise to the various challenges, physical, mental and tactical. It is a thrilling feeling to be swept along on a tide of adrenalin, a juggernaut of conviction – even more exhilarating if, like me, you are by nature a fairly pessimistic person, usually expecting things to go against you. Yet if you are strong-willed enough in training, in net practice, and in the match itself, things will often go your way. Not only must you always expect to get a wicket, but you must bowl to that purpose. A fast bowler's job is not to play a batsman in, but to blast him out with sheer aggression or tactical ingenuity. He must always attack, both in his line of delivery and field-placing. There is no point in bowling a proper line to a good batsman – well up to the bat, trying to beat him with speed through the air or late movement – if there are insufficient fielders round the bat for any edged stroke. You must come to terms with snicks through the slips to the boundary and the edges that do not go to hand. You will give away runs by attacking, but you will also take wickets: 4 for 60 is always preferable to 1 for 30 in the same number of overs. Other bowlers of different styles may have to keep the score down, but not the speed merchant. He is the strike weapon, the man who should never worry about conceding four runs an over as long as he keeps beating the bat.

A strong will. Natural ability. Luck. Good control. Fitness. Stamina. Guts. The intelligence to take and sift through advice. Pride. Optimism. That is all you need to be a fast bowler. Your ability to get near all those qualities will determine how far you go in the game. It was the first thing I ever bothered to work hard at, and everything else in my life has stemmed from that dedication.

2
THE BOWLING
ACTION

Compared with techniques associated with other sports, fast bowling is a very unnatural thing. Most sports are played with both eyes and chest focusing on the opponent or ball, yet cricket is basically a sideways-on game, with batsman and bowler at an angle of 90 degrees to each other. Urgent, split-second realignment of body is needed by a batsman to deal with the delivered ball, but the greatest physical strain is on the bowler, especially those who put great power into delivering the ball as fast as possible. The greater the effort at delivery, the faster the speed.

How can someone learn to run at about 20 mph to project a 6½-oz cricket ball at 80 mph? Fundamentally, the fast bowler has to co-ordinate his leg, arm and trunk movements to enable him to bring up his bowling arm from behind his back and over his head at such a speed that he is at his fastest at the moment of letting the ball go. He should have a well-ordered approach to the wicket, building up to a speed that will enable him comfortably to twist his body into a side-on position just before delivery. A high action and strong follow-through completes the picture. The most vital part is bodyswing – the ability to turn the trunk back from the sideways position to face the batsman at the moment of delivery in the shortest possible time. That gives the element of explosiveness all fast bowlers need in their delivery.

So much for the textbook, ideal fast bowler's action – and I hasten to add that anyone fortunate enough to achieve it is well on the way to becoming a high-class performer. The textbook version puts less physical strain on the bowler, enables him to exercise more control over his deliveries and gives him a greater chance of achieving extreme speed. Yet few are perfect in bowling actions, as in all walks of life. My own action is a coach's nightmare in technical terms, although I do redeem by managing to rotate my trunk through 90 degrees to deliver the ball. My run-up is not smooth enough, and my left leg does not brace as it hits the ground just before the right arm comes whirring over to deliver the ball. I am too open-chested when releasing the ball, and when my rhythm has deserted me I have to rely simply on my bowling arm, rather than my shoulders, to put speed into the delivery. Yet it usually feels right to me. Somehow I can bowl fast while more talented men with superb actions cannot. Many great fast bowlers have been equally idiosyncratic yet the results were impressive. No one would say Mike Procter's 'wrong-foot' action was ideal, yet he baffled a generation of batsmen by swinging the ball prodigiously through the air at high speed, despite delivering the ball unorthodoxly. Jeff Thomson – with his slinging method of catapulting the ball like a javelin thrower – looked very unorthodox, but he was capable of devastating speed and unplayable lift off the pitch. It all boils down to what suits the individual and possessing the commonsense to ignore the purists who try to reduce your firepower by turning you into a textbook bowler without the flair to bowl fast.

Apart from a few modifications, my bowling action has remained the same since I was 15, way back in the days when I just ran up and hurled it down in second-eleven games at school. Despite the strain on my physique, and the mutterings of well-intentioned coaches, I have proved to my own satisfaction that fast bowling is a matter of instinct that you refine as you get older and progress in the game. There are endless ways to tinker with the existing mechanism, but if you can bowl fast with the basic model do not allow yourself to be talked into a complete overhaul. You are one of the lucky breed. It is terribly difficult to hang on to the ability to bowl fast while refining the action to ensure that the ball goes in the right area. English first-class cricket is littered with tragic examples of naturally talented fast bowlers who allowed themselves to be talked into changing their action, rather than continue to be unorthodox while working on the finer points. If you know in your heart that things are fundamentally wrong, take advice and think about drastic alterations. Otherwise be strong-willed and concentrate on channelling your natural assets in the right direction.

If you stop to analyse the ingredients that make someone bowl fast, the results are fascinating. Dennis Lillee once commissioned an expert in physiology and fitness to do just that. These were his findings:

1. RUN-UP contributes 19 per cent
2. LEG ACTION and HIP ROTATION contributes 23 per cent
3. TRUNK MOVEMENT and SHOULDER ROTATION contributes 11 per cent
4. ARM ACTION contributes 42 per cent
5. HAND MOVEMENT contributes 5 per cent

The ability to bring the bowling arm over at high speed is therefore by far the most important asset according to scientific tests. The other interesting conclusion for me is that fast bowlers cannot be strictly categorized – one may be more impressive in his run-up, another may be better at hip rotation, a third could follow through more powerfully. No two bowlers are the same, we can only glean guidelines from the top-class performers and assess their performances.

My bowling action is a mixture of the unconventional and the orthodox – mostly the former. Just before I leap into the delivery stride, I size up the target with my right arm: sometimes this habit makes me grip the ball too tightly in case I drop it. I think my delivery leap is satisfactory, my left arm guiding my balance. On the way down from the leap, I revert to the unorthodox with my arms and legs a jumble at strange angles – I also fail to look over my left arm, not least because it is over my head at that stage! My right foot is not parallel to the bowling crease and my left leg does not brace to take the strain of delivery. Yet I do contrive to force my body round as much as possible just before delivery and this final thrust, allied to a flexible wrist movement, helps me to produce speed. My follow-through is a powerful one, although I do worry about getting an umpire's warning for running on to the pitch.

Hardly an action from the fast bowler's coaching manual, yet, with minor modifications, it has remained the same since I was fifteen. The moral must be that you should stick with an action that feels natural as long as you can bowl fast.

THE RUN-UP

A quick bowler needs to be going fast when he arrives at the bowling crease. The speed of his run should allow him to get enough bodyswing to turn his trunk sideways, then back again to deliver the ball. When he wants to bowl a really fast one, he gets extra acceleration from the last few strides, so that he can turn his trunk even more quickly at delivery. The idea of the run-up is to set yourself up at the crease in a perfectly balanced position just before releasing the ball. A gradual build-up of speed is necessary, so that top speed is reached three or four strides before delivery, with the momentum maintained until the ball is bowled.

Smoothness, balance and speed are essential for the fast bowler's run-up. Yet the speed must be there at the right time: one of the common failings among young fast bowlers is that they start sprinting at the beginning of their run and have to try to maintain the sprint all the way to the crease. This is an awful waste of energy and usually results in the bowler straining during those last few crucial strides. Nor should they sprint halfway through, only to decelerate near the crease – that will lead to a loss of speed in delivery. In every class of cricket, you can see people running up faster than they bowl. This is because not enough thought has been given to the run-up.

Length of run-up

As a general principle, a run-up should be long enough to produce speed and to enable the bowler to settle into a rhythm before letting the ball go as fast as he can. A strong man does not need a particularly long run to generate pace, that will come in the body movement at delivery, but someone like myself needs a long run to generate momentum and pace. Balance and co-ordination are such elusive things for me – halfway through my run, I can tell if I am firing on all cylinders and I know whether the delivery is going to be a fast one or just a medium-pace 'lollipop'. I have to concentrate desperately hard on retaining or regaining my rhythm.

Although most fast bowlers need a lengthy run-up to produce speed, I do feel that many of us run too far to finish up bowling medium-pace. In most cases, we are to blame at Test level. The youngsters see us haring in from 35 yards and try to emulate us – the same thing happened to me as a youngster when I would rush home from school, draw the blinds and watch the Tests on television. In my own defence, I would maintain that I need a long run because I am just not muscular enough to achieve high pace from a shorter distance, and at least I manage to bowl fast after all the effort. I do wish, however, that schoolboys and club cricketers would concentrate on the vital parts of a run-up and delivery. I would have thought that a lad under 18 should not run more than 25 yards; because he is not properly developed, the consequent physical pressure will hamper his bowling if he runs any further.

At some stage in all our careers, we have to decide how long our run-up should be. Generally, I would say that it should be as long as you like, provided it feels natural, that you are not overstretched physically, and, most important of all, the end-product is a fast delivery. When I was a boy, I would run up and bowl in my back garden to my father and brother without a thought about how I got to the crease. The day arrived when I was too big for the back garden, so we graduated to the local recreation ground. I simply marked out where to start my run, and then proceeded as far as I wanted before releasing the ball. It was simply a case of what felt natural to me. I would recommend the same thing to a youngster. Take a friend out with you to a playing field and ask him to mark the place where you delivered the ball. Pace out the distance between start and finish of the run-up and also how many paces taken. Remember which foot you started off with on your run-up and make sure you take off on the same one in the nets or in games. If your stride pattern varies each time, do it ten or 12 times to establish an average. Balance yourself after a couple of strides, then graduate to a run, and bowl when the moment feels right. Once your left foot strikes accurately in the region of the mark, you have a run-up. Only after a lot of practice in the open field should you try it out in the nets – things like stumps, and a confined space in a net can be disconcerting unless the basics have been assimilated.

Approaching the crease and avoiding the stutters

Once you have worked out the length of your run, it is time to think about the way you get to the crease, how you can approach smoothly, accelerating at the right time. In this respect, I envy the West Indian fast bowlers who seem to float on air as they run in – their natural litheness means they are smooth, co-ordinated and moving with deceptive speed.

Many fast bowlers are amazed to be told by a coach that their run-up is a mess, that they stutter along when they thought it was balanced and integrated. We all get afflicted by the stutters at some time – when somehow you fail to take the proper strides, break into a pitter-patter and arrive at the crease off-balance. Because you are so wrapped up in the actual mechanics of bowling, it is easy to overlook the fact that your stride pattern is completely awry.

Proof that even international fast bowlers should keep trying to improve their technique. Although I cannot alter the way I bowl, I have realised for some time that there was room for improvement in my run-up. My right arm used to hang down from my body as I ran in, with the result that the trailing arm sometimes unbalanced me. On the 1982-83 England tour to Australia, I worked out a new way of running in: I managed to hold my right arm in the textbook fashion and, as a result, I felt more relaxed and my run-up was much smoother. I also found that I did not grip the ball so tightly on the way in –

gone were the worries about dropping it in mid-sprint! Consequently it was easier to maintain the right kind of finger pressure on the ball just before delivery, thereby helping me to control the seam's movement off the pitch. Although my movements in the instant before delivery are still rather jumbled and unorthodox, my new approach to the wicket helps me get in the right position to cock the wrist and use my height. My improved balance also makes it easier for me to run off the wicket after delivery to avoid a warning from the umpires for scuffing up the pitch.

I can suggest two ways of sorting out your run-up. The first way is with your eyes closed. This sounds daft, I know, but not if you realise that a proper run-up is an instinctive thing. Go out into a field where there are no obstacles in the way and mark out your run-up and delivery distance. Close your eyes, start with your usual foot and proceed to walk a couple of paces, then break into your run. Do it at about three-quarters speed, count your paces and let the ball go when you think it is right to do so. Keep your eyes closed all the time and keep the head straight as you run. You will be surprised how rarely you stutter during that 'blind' run-up. If a friend can stand nearby to confirm you are not bowling no-balls, then so much the better.

I also recommend long-jump training. The board the long-jumper aims for can be likened to the bowling crease for the fast bowler. Timing, balance and controlled speed are vital to both athletes. Long-jump training helps you time the sprint and stops you overstraining in those last few strides. Whatever you do, try not to look down as you run in – that will put you off balance when you arrive at the wicket. Unless the head is still and upright, your body will be thrown out of rhythm and you will spray the ball about most of the time.

Try to run in as straight as possible. That is something I have never been able to master, although my run-up is not as curved as it used to be. I was a regular England bowler before I heeded the advice of my captain, Tony Greig, and straightened out my run. He pointed out that if you run in from an angle the ball tends to follow the direction of the curve. In my case, that meant my stock ball was the inswinger, the wrong delivery to dismiss high-class batsmen. I reduced the bend in my approach to the wicket, and in the process began to bowl more outswingers, with immediate success. It is terribly difficult to change your habits from over a decade, but there is no doubt in my mind that a straight run gives you more chance to be balanced when you deliver the ball.

So much stems from a proper run-up. Every great fast bowler I can think of looked superb in his approach to the crease, totally in control of himself. I am afraid that cricketers are not precise enough about their run-ups, compared with long-jumpers or javelin throwers, yet we have to be equally exact in the positioning of our feet. We have to run about 30 yards – most of that at speed – and then compose ourselves to deliver the ball from a point behind a crease to avoid being no-balled. Yet we rely on pacing out our run-up, ignoring the fact that, some days, our strides are larger or smaller. It is all rather inexact and I wonder whether we should be more precise in measuring out a run-up. Why not carry around a piece of string that measures the exact length? I am sure the purists would deplore such a practice and there is no doubt that allowance should be made for bowling uphill or downhill, yet I believe there is no substitute for knowing precisely where your feet should be landing as you run in. Anything I can do to smooth out my run-up is welcomed, and I am sure that applies to most fast bowlers.

The 'no-ball' problem

For a fast bowler, a natural sequel to an ineffective run-up is no-ball trouble. I have suffered greatly from this over the years and sometimes it really gets to me and ruins that delicate balance between commitment and control. It is the biggest worry for a fast bowler, totally undermining confidence so that you come to feel like the hurdler who knocks over each hurdle. You have to be very positive about no-ball trouble and accept it as an occupational hazard, even though it gives the batsman a free hit, costs you and the team some runs and mortifies you if you take a wicket just after you hear the umpire shout 'no-ball'.

The law states that you have to keep some part of the front foot behind the batting crease at the point of delivery. When no-ball problems start, the instinctive thing to do is take back your marker a foot or two at the start of your run-up. Try to avoid that – it only confuses you and destroys your rhythm. Take a foot back at the bowling crease instead, so that you land a little further back from the danger area while still keeping your run-up intact.

You have to talk yourself back into the groove when you start bowling no-balls, or, failing that, just accept them. I appreciate that sounds like bad cricket, but the alternative is a loss of concentration and speed. The greatest performance of my Test career came when I was having terrible trouble with no-balls. It was at Leeds in 1981 when I took 8 for 43 to give England that incredible win over Australia when we seemed dead and buried. Out of their total of 111, I bowled 14 no-balls. I would never have forgiven myself if they had sneaked home, courtesy of my defects, but I decided that my rhythm was so good that day that I must not compromise. I accepted I would stray over the line on occasions, but the alternative was friendly medium-pace. We had to win and I had to take chances.

I would advise a young fast bowler not to worry too much about no-balls. Provided he is intelligent enough to work on the problem eventually, he should concentrate instead on getting the basics right and leave the decisions to the umpire. Whatever happens, do not allow yourself to be sidetracked; if you are worried about where your feet are landing, you will not bowl fast that day. An occasional no-ball will always happen when a genuine fast bowler puts in extra effort and overstretches himself at the bowling crease.

THE DELIVERY

Having sorted out his run-up to his satisfaction, the fast bowler now has to deliver the ball. To get the best results, he has to turn his body side-on to the batsman. That takes a conscious effort, especially after a long run to the wicket, but the extra exertion increases the wicket-taking potential, enabling the bowler to deliver the ball at various angles and at high speed. Here are the crucial ingredients for the classical fast bowler's delivery in order of sequence:

1. A final leap
2. The back foot is planted parallel to the bowling crease
3. The bowling arm is taken to a slightly bent position level with the bowler's forehead and the wrist is cocked
4. The front (left) arm is thrust high in the air
5. The eyes look over the front shoulder at the target
6. The back is arched
7. The body is twisted at 90 degrees to the batsman, with the left shoulder pointing towards him
8. The right arm is extended back and then begins its forward swing
9. The left arm starts swinging forward and down
10. The front (left) leg braces when hitting the ground and points towards fine-leg
11. The ball is released at speed with hand and fingers behind it
12. The bowling arm brushes the right ear and chest on the way down
13. The weight goes forward and the right leg comes past the front leg
14. The bowling arm follows the left arm on to the left side of the body
15. The left arm extends behind the body, taking the bowling arm and shoulders through with it
16. Follow through vigorously in the direction of third man

I liken the fast bowler's delivery to the cocking and firing of a rifle. The left arm that is thrust high into the air drags the body up and acts as the sighter at the end of the rifle. The right arm is the hammer, cocked back, ready to release the ball in tandem with the left arm going downwards. The result is a controlled explosion of power and accuracy if everything is in harmony. If the timing is just a little out, then the ball can go anywhere.

That final leap is very important. Just before releasing the ball, you need to be as far off the ground as possible. A high arm action gives you that extra bounce and the ability to make the ball rise sharply, an invaluable asset on a slow pitch.

Dennis Lillee's glorious delivery leap underlines the importance of long-jump training to a fast bowler if he is suffering from a lack of co-ordination and rhythm. Like a long-jumper, a fast bowler has to run a long way and time his take-off to precision. Look at the height of Lillee's left knee (considering he has run in at speed) and note how the left palm to the sky helps drag up his body to give him height in the delivery. The wrist is cocked to impart extra pace and the grip on the ball is loose, yet controlled. A marvellous athlete and performer.

The fact that I deliver the ball from a height of about eight feet is one of my greatest assets and helps compensate for some of my technical defects. Even though my left knee collapses when hitting the ground and I have to rely on my left hip to take the strain, I can still get my arm coming over from a great height because of that final leap.

Always look over your front shoulder at the batsman just before your delivery stride begins: it helps you aim properly. Fix your eyes on the off stump and keep the head still. Throw that left palm to the sky and wind yourself up to deliver the ball with venom. Get those hips moving dynamically, from side-on through a 90-degree turn. The hips should turn just before the left leg hits the ground, braced for the impact. As the bowling arm comes from behind the trunk, the right side of the body is released – this means that the right hip will come

How to launch yourself into the delivery stride. Michael Holding, Rodney Hogg and Ian Botham have all ensured that the upper body is leaning back from the waist, like a coiled spring. As a result, they are in excellent positions to get maximum effect and speed from the delivery stride. Note in each case the right foot: it is parallel to the crease in the textbook manner, giving every chance of a side–on action that will help them bowl the outswinger.

round as the bowling arm swings down and the back changes from its arched position to a more rounded one. The bodyswing starts and, with the release of the right side, the shoulders jerk back to bring the chest facing the batsman. This jerking of hips and shoulders helps the right arm to accelerate in its downward swing – remember the bowling arm must come down with the greatest possible speed. The bowling arm performs a complete circle as the weight goes forward on to the braced left leg. The rotation of the hips enables the back leg to go in front of the left just after the ball is delivered, and the bowler follows through away from the centre of the pitch. A vigorous, positive follow-through is very important: do not clip it, because you will lose pace. It is part of the action and a good follow-through stems from a final solid thrust in the delivery. If you have done that properly, you should need a few steps to regain balance and a few more to slow down. If you stop too soon, you will lose rhythm and put an unnecessary strain on ankles and knees. Make yourself follow through in an arc that takes you away from the wicket as soon as you can. I am often at fault in this respect, due to my keeness to get as close to the stumps as possible, so that I can bowl the one that runs away from the batsman. Although my new run-up has helped, I find it very difficult to veer away from the 'business area' of the wicket immediately after delivering the ball – those wonky knees again! I need time to follow through naturally without any braking or abrupt changes of direction which would trouble my knees. That is my problem, though, and I accept umpires' criticisms in this matter, and would advise any fast bowler not to follow my example.

Some youngsters often fall over in their enthusiasm during their follow-through. That is a fault in the right direction: it means they are committed to giving their all, striving for that explosiveness in delivery. I have often seen that happen in Tests and, although some get a cheap laugh when an illustrious fast bowler falls flat on his face, it proves that he is not just going through the motions.

I suppose the smooth, finished product of the high-class fast bowler must make many schoolboys and club cricketers green with envy. They probably look at the Test opening bowlers and wonder how they ever achieved such a standard. All I can say is that innumerable fast bowlers have played many times for their country with distinction, yet they were technically inferior in some important areas of their craft. A man like Dennis Lillee comes along just once in a generation; the rest of us have to soldier on, relying on hard work and common sense, rather than genius. Many an illustrious fast bowler has failed to brace his left leg at the vital moment, or bowled with a round-arm delivery or sent down vicious bouncers or swingers off the 'wrong foot'. Some wasted part of their run-ups, others curtailed their follow-throughs or failed to get totally side-on.

The fast bowler must use his height to get the maximum bounce – a priceless ingredient when the wicket is slow and the fast bowler is the only one who can extract life from it. Malcolm Marshall and Andy Roberts are not the biggest men ever to bowl for the West Indies, but they both realise the importance of a launching pad. In my case, the final leap enables me to deliver the ball from a height of more than eight feet.

ABOVE LEFT Kapil Dev gives the ideal example of how to size up a batsman by looking over his left shoulder. He is beautifully balanced for the delivery and he knows just where he is aiming the ball. Note the cocked wrist: a whippy, wristy action invariably compensates for a lack of physical power in the arms and shoulders.

LEFT An example of the kind of effort needed to bowl fast. Derbyshire's Paul Newman has gathered himself for that last vital thrust of the body. His left leg is correctly pointing in the direction of fine leg, allowing his body then to rotate in the approved fashion, and the leg is about to take the strain of delivery. His left arm is high enough to drag the body upwards, so that the ball will be delivered from as great a height as possible. Note the tips of the fingers on the seam with the thumb acting as a steadying influence; note also how the bowler's eyes are fixed firmly on the target.

ABOVE RIGHT Another view of the final delivery stride. Kent's Graham Dilley is dragging his body into position (note the plate on the right boot to adsorb the impact) and the left leg is about to take the strain. The body is arched back, ready to 'catapult' the ball at the batsman.

ABOVE You can judge whether a fast bowler is really putting his back into his work by watching his feet after he has delivered the ball. If they are off the ground for an instant, then the effort is being expended. Andy Roberts and Ian Botham have both done that while still managing to keep their eyes fixed on the stumps at the other end.

RIGHT In the follow-through, the left arm should take the body back as far as possible to accommodate a powerful extension of the bowling arm. Here Norman Cowans demonstrates a supple, co-ordinated follow-through.

Imran Khan gets his speed from a long run and an impressive strength in his upper torso. He has developed his arm, chest and shoulder muscles to give him speed through strength, rather than co-ordination. He may lack certain classical assets – for example, he does not look over his left arm just before delivery – but he more than compensates with a swift arm movement, a braced left leg and a whippy, powerful follow-through.

A graphic example of how a fast bowler can get everything into his delivery. Geoff Lawson uses all his height in a tremendous final leap while avoiding too tight a grip on the ball. The left leg is thrown out far enough to accommodate a long drag of the body (note the steel cap on the right boot) and the right arm goes a long way down to ensure he gets the fullest arc possible to gather speed and momentum to deliver the ball. From a strong, braced left leg, the trunk swivels through a wide area and the bowling arm comes right over the top. The follow-through is absolutely dynamic – at one stage it looks as if all that effort will make him topple over!

Do not worry if you fall down in certain areas of technique: keep your eyes open and watch those who seem to have all the necessary attributes. Go and watch the great fast bowlers in action if you can – television distorts the action and cannot do justice to all the components that are needed to bowl fast. Watch the play from a side-on position, examine how a quick bowler runs to the wicket, how high he leaps before delivery and how far he follows through after releasing the ball. At close of play or the end of an innings, join the throng watching the groundsman and his staff cleaning up the wicket, but do not stand there listening to others forecasting the game's result and hazarding guesses about how the wicket will play on the morrow. Go and look at the imprints made by the fast bowler's feet in his run-up; you should be able to see them clearly all the way from start to bowling crease if he has been bowling properly. His feet ought to have landed in the same place throughout the day. Examine the bowling crease: if there is a fair-sized hole, then the fast bowler has been trying hard. Observe how far he has followed through; whether he has used the extremities of the crease to vary his line.

If you are keen and observant enough, then you cannot fail to improve your technique by analysing those fast bowlers currently at the top of their tree. Gain inspiration from them – try to run up like one and deliver the ball like another. There is nothing wrong in trying to copy the best. When I was a boy, my hero was Brian Statham. I watched him on the television and slavishly imitated his deceptively easy approach to the wicket and tried to match his deadly accuracy. I really thought I bowled like him for a long time! No one disabused me of the notion that I was the Southern Statham, yet can you imagine two fast bowlers more dissimilar? It did not matter: Statham's stature had inspired me and made me want to be a fast bowler. I loved to watch cricket because of him and, as a result, I picked up all sorts of knowledge.

If you are lucky enough to have the classic fast bowler's action, then the sky really is the limit, provided you possess the other necessary qualities of self-discipline, intelligence, bravery and an adequate physique. You must never take your action for granted, however: like all smooth machines, it occasionally needs a tune-up. Keep reminding yourself of the basics. Stop that head lolling around from side to side as you run in, look straight ahead all the time, get those legs pumping to provide momentum, then leap high enough to give you time to turn side-on before landing. Make the body work the arm to boost speed of delivery. Throw the left palm to the sky, always look at the off stump from over the left shoulder and slam that bowling arm down. Make sure you follow through with power and purpose. When the machine is ticking over nicely, fast bowling can be a wonderful stimulus, full reward for all the hours spent in polishing up the technique. Of course it is difficult to thrust yourself into a side-on position when running in at about 20 mph, but if you manage to fuse all the elements at the right time, life becomes even more difficult for the batsman.

Common faults in a fast bowler's action

1. A lack of a consistent run-up that gradually accelerates and allows for a satisfactory jump off the left foot.

---

2. Not enough height and rotation on the jump.

---

3. Failing to land with the right foot parallel to the bowling crease – caused by insufficient turning of the shoulders at the moment of take-off.

---

4. No arching of the back and a failure to lean the body away from the batsman.

---

5. Bowling off the wrong foot, caused by a combination of (2) and (4) above. This usually leads to the bowler's right foot pointing down the pitch.

---

6. The left arm not climbing high enough.

---

7. The head not looking down the pitch from behind the front arm.

---

8. The front foot splaying to the off side after landing too wide.

---

9. Failure to thrust down the front arm at the moment of delivery: this prevents the bowling arm from being as high as possible.

---

10. An inadequate follow-through.

---

11. A lack of concentration – failing to fix the eyes and mind on the appropriate length to be bowled.

3

SWING AND SEAM BOWLING

The basic function of a fast bowler is to get the ball down the other end as quickly as possible, in a direction that will cause problems to batsmen. If, in addition to his speed, he has the ability to make the ball swing through the air or deviate off the pitch, a fast bowler can be a formidable prospect. Should the bowler lack that extra pace which separates him from the rest, he can still be a major weapon in the bowling line-up if he has learned to make the ball swing or seam off the wicket. Let us examine the differences between the three types of bowlers.

The fast bowler aims for speed through the air, a rare commodity. He is an attacker who does not swing the ball all that much because he bowls at a speed which is less affected by the aerodynamic forces that make a ball swing. A tough proposition on any surface, provided he is in control of the delicate mechanism of his action: so much can go wrong because of the need to generate top speed.

The seamer is slower in pace and relies on subtle changes of action and hand movement to make the ball alter its course after pitching. He should be able to bowl the yorker and the bouncer and ought to be fully in control of his action because he does not need to steam into the crease. For that reason he should never deliver a no-ball: it is a free hit to a good batsman, who will have time to adjust and play an attacking shot. Line and length become crucial: whilst a fast bowler can take wickets with a fast full-toss, a seamer has no such luck. A good seamer will be able to seal up one end, bowling short of a length with enough nip off the pitch to tie down a batsman, giving his captain enough time to rest his fast bowlers without giving away too many runs. A seamer comes into his own in English conditions, where the dampish green wickets allow the ball to bite.

The swing bowler pitches the ball further up and is more attacking. When conditions favour him – a humid atmosphere and plenty of cloud cover – he can be devastating, especially if he possesses a quicker ball to give him variety. He relies on changes of pace, using the full width of the crease and alterations in line to bowl the outswinger and the inswinger. A class swing bowler can make a batsman look stupid as he essays a flowing off-drive, only to be bowled leg stump between bat and pad! His swing can be spotted early – therefore the swing bowler who can make the ball curve as late as possible is very fortunate.

SWING BOWLING

I imagine everyone is very surprised the first time he manages to get a ball to dip through the air and wonders what he did to cause it. Sometimes it is just a freak of nature, but that does not apply when practised at the top level. The art of making the ball deviate through the air from leg to off (outswinger) or off to leg (inswinger) is an exact science: when demonstrated by men like Dennis Lillee, swing bowling at speed is wonderful to watch.

A cricket ball swings because of aerodynamics. A slight alteration in air

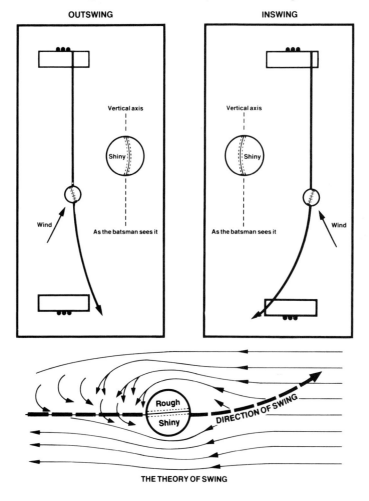

OUTSWING

INSWING

Vertical axis

Shiny

As the batsman sees it

Wind

Vertical axis

Shiny

As the batsman sees it

Wind

Rough

Shiny

DIRECTION OF SWING

THE THEORY OF SWING

The right and wrong way to deliver the ball. Keep that arm as high as possible, to enable the seam to hit the pitch first and to get sufficient bounce to trouble the batsman. A round-arm action usually ensures the minimum of bounce and 'hitting the seam' becomes a lottery. Accuracy is also forfeited.

The right and wrong way to hold the ball – the proper method is with the meat of the thumb and knuckle part of the fingers. Do not push the ball too far into the fingers – the idea is to retain control but not sacrifice speed.

pressures on the two sides of a cricket ball somehow manages to create a distinct swing in its flight down the wicket. When a new ball – shiny on both sides – is taken, a roughness soon develops on one side of the ball if the seam is pointed most of the time in the right direction. Once a side is rougher than the other, an air flow is created which is different from that on the other side; a sideways force makes the ball swing. As the ball gets rougher – after about 12 overs – the flow becomes the same on either side and it stops swinging. That is when the bowler should polish it on one particular side. Choose the one with the least amount of lettering on it – giving you the greatest area of leather. The smooth layer of air on the shiny part somehow breaks away from the ball faster than the air on the rough side. Thus the ball swings in the direction of the rough side. So for the inswinger the shiny part points to the off side; for the outswinger the shiny part points to the on side. After those early overs, the seam must be in a vertical position when the ball is delivered to ensure late swing in either direction. A high arm action is important to keep the ball well up to the batsman – there is no point in bowling good, swinging deliveries if they pitch short and sit up to be smashed.

The vital part of swing bowling concerns the way you let the ball go. The danger is that the ball will not swing at all, or will swing too little or even too early in its flight to bother a batsman. The ball should be gripped in a specific way, with the index and middle fingers on top and the thumb underneath, resting on the seam. The position of the two fingers alters in the case of the outswinger and the inswinger, but at all times the tips of the fingers should be used: if the ball is gripped too tightly in the hand, crucial control will be lost. At the point of delivery the hand should be directly behind the seam and should not cut down on either side; this causes a loss of pace and also means the ball will not deviate in the way you want. The wrist should be cocked to deliver the ball – this gives extra pace and also under-spin which helps to give late swing. If you have a naturally whippy wrist action you should be quite a handful with swinging deliveries because the extra under-spin imparted to the ball will make it dip alarmingly.

THE OUTSWINGER

The outswinger is traditionally the ball that dismisses the best players. The aim is to make the batsman play at a ball he thinks he has got covered, but make him snick a late-swinging delivery to the slips or wicket-keeper. Ideally the outswinger should start its flight on line with the leg stump and swing to just outside the off stump by the time the batsman plays at it. Make the batsman play at the ball: it is wasteful to bowl a beautiful outswinger that is ignored because it started out on the middle stump and swung too early.

For the outswinger, the ball is gripped between the index and middle fingers with the shiny side pointing towards leg and the seam pointing slightly towards the slips. A side-on delivery is critical, so all the ingredients for that are brought to bear – the right foot parallel to the crease, the left palm pointing to the sky, the bowler looking over his left shoulder and the front leg coming across the body to take the strain. Eyes fixed on the target, the left arm tucked in close to its side of the body and right shoulder and body come across the pivot of the front foot. The bowling arm should be high but, if possible, a little round-armed. This will help send the ball in the right direction – towards the slips – and make it easier for the bowler's right hand to finish down the left side of his body. The ball should be delivered from near to the stumps, to enable the swing to start close to the leg stump – if you deliver an outswinger from the extremity of the crease, the chances are that it will swing harmlessly away. Just try to bowl straight at leg stump and hope the swing and a good body action does the rest. Do not forget that vigorous follow-through . . . you need pace allied to the swing.

If you are a swing bowler rather than a quick one who occasionally swings it, you will want to be able to bowl a faster outswinger when necessary. Perhaps you operate off an eight-pace run – and very sensible too if you are not that quick – so you will have to put more into your body action for the quicker one. The long arc of the bowling arm should increase the pace, especially if the right arm follows the left arm round the left side of the body after the ball has been delivered.

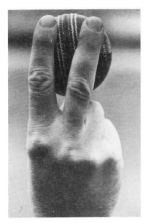

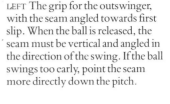

LEFT The grip for the outswinger, with the seam angled towards first slip. When the ball is released, the seam must be vertical and angled in the direction of the swing. If the ball swings too early, point the seam more directly down the pitch.

CENTRE LEFT Dennis Lillee and Ian Botham have both got into the classical position to bowl the outswinger at speed. They are about to land with the right foot in the correct position to ensure a full rotation of the hips, their final leap has given them enough height to generate bounce and they are leaning back a little to size up the target.

BELOW The perfect seam bowler's action, courtesy of Richard Hadlee. After an economical run-up his main work is done in his classical delivery style: the right foot is parallel to the crease, he looks over his shoulder at the batsman, the right hip comes round at the moment of delivery while the left foot points towards gully. After delivery, the right arm follows through strongly. The ideal action to enable the bowler to deliver the outswinger.

THE INSWINGER

Some of the principles of the inswinger are the exact opposite to those of the outswinger. The normal pace-bowler's action gives outswing, not inswing, so you have to act against some of the usual principles. The bulk of the wickets obtained by the outswinger are catches, but with the inswinger you generally try to bowl the batsman out. The inswinger should be aimed to start outside the off stump and dip in to hit the stumps. It should be delivered from wide out on the crease, with the shiny side of the ball facing the off side and the seam pointing towards leg slip. A high action is again necessary but from a more front-on position. You open up your body just a little and instead of thrusting the left palm to the sky, it goes only three-quarters of the way and your head looks underneath at the target. The back foot is not quite parallel to the crease and the left leg is splayed out towards the off side, rather than fine leg as for the outswinger. When releasing the ball, the body is completely front-on to the batsman, the bowling arm is angled to slant the ball inwards and the front foot comes round towards a point looking directly down the wicket. On the follow-through, the bowling arm completes its downward movement on the right-hand side of the body, rather than the left-hand side as for the outswinger.

As you have to make clear adjustments to bowl the two different swinging deliveries, it is advisable to restrict the changes. If you are lucky enough to possess a natural side-on bowling action, you should be able to bowl the outswinger without any real problems; you would then rightly worry about losing your fluency of movement for the sake of learning to bowl the inswinger. Certainly the basic action for the inswinger requires less effort, concentration and style and it would be easy to fall into bad habits and take up bowling inswingers most of the time. Yet if you can manage to bowl both deliveries with a basically similar action, you will be doubly lucky – the existing impressive machine will remain unimpaired and you will keep the batsman guessing about the swing. At the point of delivery it becomes fairly obvious which one is going to be bowled, but by that time it is usually too late for the batsman to adjust – you would be surprised how few batsmen watch the swing-bowler's feet. If you can perfect the inswinger and outswinger with little change in action you should reap a harvest of wickets. You will be able to open up a batsman's stance for the expected inswinger, only to make the ball swing away from his bat so that he edges it to the slips, with his feet nowhere. He can be clean bowled by an inswinging yorker while trying to hit you past mid-off. Or better still – bowl him an occasional straight one that does nothing. Very satisfying!

LEFT The grip for the inswinger, with the seam angled towards fine leg. The inswinger is bowled with a more open-chested delivery than the outswinger and the front foot lands wider towards the off side.

CENTRE Brian Statham's high, slightly open-chested delivery action which meant that he tended to bowl the inswinger. Note that he is looking inside his left arm and that his head is steady as a rock, with his eyes fixed firmly on the target.

BELOW Although my basic action has remained the same since my schooldays, I have tried to iron out little technical faults wherever possible, despite my unorthodox style. In the early part of my first-class career I was very off-balance in the delivery stride, which meant I bowled too much down the leg side. My left arm was too high and failing to steady the body and I gripped the ball far too tightly. Eventually (right) I got much nearer to the stumps and a lower left arm balanced my body to enable me to use my height and be in a position to know where I was delivering the ball. I learned how to use the tips of my fingers on the seam, so that – although I was still a little too chest-on – I could rely on the seam to move the ball away from the bat. In the early days, my obvious technical defects meant my stock ball was the inswinger.

THE SLOWER BALL

Another weapon in the swing-bowler's armoury is the slower ball. The idea is to confuse the batsman with the change in pace and get him playing too early, either giving a catch or finding himself clean bowled by playing over the top of the delivery. If it is well-concealed and used with discretion, the slower ball is very effective; if overused or poorly delivered, it usually means four runs to the batsman.

There are many ways of mastering the slower ball and ultimately it depends on which way best suits the individual. One obvious way is to deliver the ball from a yard further back, but it is an easy one for the batsman to spot and might also disrupt your run-up. Another way is to slow down the bowling arm so that the ball takes longer to travel the same distance. The problem here is that you can concentrate so intently on making the ball go straight that it might come out too slowly from the hand. I think the easiest way is to hold the ball deep in the hand, rather than with the fingers, and then deliver it normally. The ball is taken right into the palm with the thumb to one side, rather than underneath the seam. You might try the half-ball grip: hold the ball on just one half and deliver it with the usual action. It then tends to slip out of the side of the hand, rather than through the force of fingers and wrist. The one-finger grip gives an even slower delivery: hold the ball with just the index finger on the top of the seam, with the thumb at the bottom. The thrust of only one finger behind the ball at delivery slows down its flight. If you have enough confidence in your ability, you could even try bowling a leg-break or an off-break at the end of your normal run – that should confuse the wicket-keeper, never mind the batsman! Finally, there is the 'knuckle' ball: clench all four knuckles of your fingers round the ball, use your normal action and at the moment of delivery release the ball with a splaying of the fingers. This is a very difficult one to master, but immensely pleasing if you get it right.

Practice is essential to master a particular slower ball that suits your action. Do not use it in a game until you are confident you are in control of it; even then try it out against mediocre batsmen first. A good player loves poorly disguised and directed slower balls and you might end up discouraged from using it. Perhaps you may not take many wickets with it, but at least the batsman will know you are an intelligent bowler and you will keep him on his toes, not knowing what to expect. A good bowler of any type wants seeds of doubt sown into a batsman's mind as early as possible, but never forget the surprise factor: do not overuse the slower ball.

Three ways to bowl the slower ball. *Left* Hold the ball deeper into the palm. *Centre* Place the fingers across rather than alongside the seam, using the thumb for balance underneath. *Right* Grip the ball with just one finger – the thrust of only one finger will reduce the speed considerably.

You will also find that the slower ball swings, albeit discernibly. Wind-tunnel tests have shown that a cricket ball does not swing above a certain speed, about 90 mph, so when the ball is delivered it does not swing initially because it is travelling too fast. As it gets near the other end of the pitch it slows down on the smooth side of the ball, making it swing in the direction of the rough side. A ball will swing more readily in humid conditions because the moist air raises the seam a little. This alters the airflow around the ball when it is in flight and the air pressures on either side of the ball act against one another, creating swing.

One further piece of advice for the swing bowler: never be afraid to bowl from round the wicket. This is particularly advisable if you are swinging the ball too far away from the batsman, so that he has time to get out of the way or adjust his stroke. If you come round the wicket, the outswinger will go across the batsman's body and he will have to play at it if pitched properly, no matter how great the swing. There is also the chance of bowling him round his legs with a quicker outswinger, where the batsman miscalculates the degree of late movement. Provided you do not lose your rhythm and control, it is always worth a few overs round the wicket if you are struggling with the conventional methods.

SEAM BOWLING

The seamer is a different animal to the swing bowler. He attacks less (unless the conditions favour him), does not favour extravagant changes of pace or direction and keeps plugging away at just short of a length. His sole aim is to 'hit the seam' – the first part of the ball to hit the pitch must be the seam, with the result that the ball will fall over to one side. If the deviation is backed up by a fair amount of pace, then so much the better because the batsman will have less time to get into a proper position. The seamer barely touches the ball at delivery, with just the first two fingers on either side of the seam and the thumb for balance; that should give you greater control and help you hit the seam. I must confess I sometimes fall down in this respect: sometimes I am so tensed up that I grip the ball too tightly and my flailing run-up has meant that unless I hang on to the ball, it might not be there when I get to the crease!

The grip for a seamer is quite straightforward. Hold the seam upright between the first two fingers and deliver it with an outswinger's action, observing all the classical disciplines. If it is delivered properly, the seam will 'bite' in that fraction of a second when it comes in contact with the pitch and will then alter its direction. It may surprise some of you to know that the seam bowler rarely knows where the ball will go after pitching. Mike Brearley once learned this to his surprise when captaining England in a Test. He told Mike Hendrick – that master of accurate seam bowling – that he wanted three in a row to move in on the batsman, followed by one that went the other way. Mike replied 'Sorry, skipper – I don't know which way it's going to go when it leaves my hand.' That is not necessarily a bad thing, because if the bowler does not know what the ball will do, what chance has the batsman got?

The ability to land the seam on target is the hallmark of class. If the ball is returned to you and there is a scuff mark on its side, then you are not bowling properly. Get rid of that scuff mark for a start: smooth over the bruise with a damp thumb and shine it up. Ignore the dull side as you want to heighten the contrast between that and the shiny area. You need to shine the ball for yourself as well as the team's swing bowler, because even if you are not managing to hit the seam you can still hope for some movement in the air from an outswinger's action. Now attend to that seam: if it has come back to you with bits of grass between the stitching, get them out. On a damp day, or if the wicket is green, earth gets clogged up in the seam, yet those are the conditions in which a seamer should excel, because the green wicket will respond to a properly directed seam. Ideally

How to use the tips of the fingers to bowl a seamer. John Snow has got everything right here: he has just enough control with his two fingers while the thumb acts simply as a steadier. A relaxed, yet controlled grip means that the ball will be released at speed, with the seam almost certain to hit the turf and deviate. Too many bowlers get tensed up and grip the ball too tightly, with the result that they lose pace and the wrong part of the ball hits the pitch first. John Snow's high arm and his steady head indicate that he is completely in control of the delivery.

the seam should stand out white against the red of the leather as the ball makes its way through the air.

If you are not hitting the seam your grip is invariably at fault, so remember that you use the tips of the fingers, not a firm grip. Bowl a proper length, do not pitch it up too far so that the bat comes in contact with the ball before it pitches. Get that bowling arm over higher. Concentrate. You may be tempted to pick at the seam and raise it up, but this is illegal and should not be attempted. I shall never forget the first time I saw that done. I was playing club cricket while still at school and this grizzled old boy was raising the seam as he walked back to his mark. He was making the ball go in all sorts of directions – no wonder, you could have cut paper with the seam by the time he had finished! Definitely the wrong thing to do.

If the seamer can manage the technique of hitting the seam, then he will be a lively proposition on wickets that give him a little assistance and can still play an important 'stock' role on good pitches where he is asked to keep the batsmen quiet. There will come the time when his arm is no longer so high and he loses that extra bit of 'nip' in the delivery. If he has managed to acquire the ability to bowl 'cutters', he will continue to be a valuable bowler.

CUTTERS

Cutters are basically spinners bowled at a fair pace and are a useful extension to a seamer's repertoire. They are particularly useful on a slow, dusty wicket when the seam does little after hitting the pitch, or when the new ball is some way off and the bowlers have to manage with a worn, ragged ball that has taken some punishment and is yielding little shine or purchase on a battered seam. The action of the hand, which comes either inside or outside the ball to impart spin, is the critical factor with cutters. Accuracy in line and length is also crucial.

To bowl the leg-cutter, the hand and wrist come inside the ball. Grip the ball, with the seam horizontal, between the top joints of the index and second fingers. The top joint of the index finger points towards eleven o'clock and the second finger towards one o'clock. The third finger should grip the ball at five o'clock while the thumb gives support and the little finger is loose. The delivery action is similar to that of the inswinger – look alongside the raised front arm just before bringing up the bowling arm. Release the ball when the bowling arm is at its highest, at which time the seam should be pointing towards gully. The cut is then imparted by pulling down the index, second and third fingers, with the wrist in the direction of gully. The resulting spin or cut should cause the ball to move from leg to off after hitting the pitch. In the follow-through, the bowling arm swings across the body and finishes in a line between the legs.

For the off-cutter, you grip the ball with the index and middle fingers close together on the seam and cut the hand and fingers down outside the ball. The bowling arm finishes on the right side of the body. For both forms of cutters, it is crucial to bring the wrist and fingers down sharply – do not roll the ball, give it a strong flick. The line for both deliveries is middle-and-off stump, just short of a length. Always aim at the stumps because the cutter does not move as much as the swinger or indeed as much as the ball that hits the seam at speed. It is preferable to bowl them with an old ball because a shiny surface makes it difficult to get a proper grip as you cut your hand down either side.

If cutters are bowled properly, they can be enormously difficult to play – in effect, they become fast leg-breaks or off-breaks. They are very hard to master and endless practice is necessary. I would advise every seam or swing bowler to try them out, but remember that a totally different hand movement is needed. Cutting the hand down the side of the ball is a bad habit for a swing or seam bowler – it gets you out of the knack of landing the seam on the pitch or of making the ball swing with a nice, high action delivered with plenty of power from the wrist. When you let the ball go without hand or fingers behind the ball, you

The grip for the leg-cutter. The middle finger is alongside the seam for maximum grip and the wrist and fingers are pulled sharply down on the left-hand side of the ball. In effect, leg-spin is imparted on the ball.

The grip for the off-cutter. It is delivered with an action similar to that for an outswinger. The wrist and fingers are brought sharply down across the seam on the right-hand side of the ball at the moment of delivery and the hand rotates in a clockwise direction.

lose the ability to swing it. I would recommend devoting some time in the nets to bowling with correct hand movements for the basic swing and seam deliveries after finishing your practice of cutters. The ability to bowl seam or swing should not be lost due to the laudable desire to extend your technical repertoire by learning how to deliver cutters.

I wish I could manage to bowl them respectably. I have experimented in some county matches when the wickets have been very slow and it needs patience and accuracy. Unfortunately my body does not go in the right direction and I lack that vital rocking motion at the delivery stride. As a fast bowler in his thirties I realize I have to adapt my style to the passage of time and I envy men like Fred Trueman and Alec Bedser who could bowl cutters at will. I remember Dennis Lillee once bowling England out on a slow, dead Melbourne wicket by cutting down his pace and bowling some perfect leg-cutters. That performance convinced me he was the greatest technician among all the fast bowlers I have ever seen. He realised the conventional weapons were useless in the conditions and he did the damage with, in effect, fast spin-bowling.

THE YORKER AND THE BOUNCER

Time to consider two other important attacking deliveries – the yorker and the bouncer. Obviously the bouncer is more dangerous in the hands of a genuine quick bowler, but if a seam or swing bowler can bowl a presentable one on rare occasions, it is worth it, if only to keep the batsman guessing. The bouncer – when used sparingly – is a legitimate delivery sent down from short of a length, designed to reach the area between the batsman's chest and just above his head. The plan is threefold – to frighten the batsman and unnerve him, to get him caught close to the wicket as he fends it off with bat or gloves, or to encourage a mistimed hook shot. I do not believe in blatant intimidation by using the bouncer but I do feel it is a perfectly reputable ploy, provided it is not overdone. I would not recommend it in school or club cricket, where often the wickets are dangerous and the batsman does not have sufficient protective clothing. The bouncer should be sent down at something faster than your normal delivery speed, because thumping it into the pitch at well short of a length can reduce its pace after it hits the pitch – if it reaches the batsman too slowly it is an innocuous, expensive error. Do not overdo its use, especially against class batsmen who are happy to see it bouncing harmlessly over their heads – that is just a waste of time and energy. Bouncers can be hard work and tactically wasteful – your captain will not be too pleased with you for getting the shine off the ball too soon by pitching it short all the time. Remember that the risk of no-balling is greatly increased when bowling bouncers, because you are putting in that little bit of extra effort in the delivery and therefore likely to stray over the line.

The yorker is a very potent weapon if used properly and at the right time. It is especially effective against those batsmen with a high backlift or who are slow on their feet. It is aimed at the base of the stumps and delivered faster than normal in the hope that it will sneak under the bat and hit the stumps. The length varies from just forward of the batting crease to the very foot of the stumps, depending on the height and backlift of the appropriate batsman. A full toss to one is a yorker to another. The fact that a ball is well pitched up increases the likelihood of swing and a chance to produce that most devastating of deliveries, the late-swinging yorker.

LINE AND LENGTH

The optimum line and length varies according to the different categories of bowler. For the genuinely quick bowler, the ideal is to get the batsman half back, half forward to a ball fractionally short of a length on the off stump. He will need to play forward in case he is trapped lbw with one that nips back off the seam; yet if the ball is just a little short, he will be uncomfortable on the front foot, worried that the ball will rear up and take the top part of the bat without giving him the chance to get out of the way. The fast bowler should avoid over-pitching but not bowl short enough to be cut or hooked. Until he enters first-class cricket, the fast bowler should not worry unduly if he fails to be bang-on target all the time; natural pace is his big advantage, not the knack of dropping the ball on a sixpence. Sometimes he will be hammered, but most of the time he will get away with it because of sheer speed.

The seamer and the swing bowler have to be more accurate because they are slower through the air and therefore more vulnerable against the confident strokemaker. The swing bowler must pitch it up to enable the ball to swing as late as possible, while the seamer has to operate in a difficult area that requires precision. If he drops it too short, his lack of real speed might mean he will be punished. If he pitches it up, he can hope for some swing, even though his technique is not all that impressive. He has to aim for the same area as the fast bowler – neither fully forward nor back – and he must also ensure that the seam hits the wicket first.

In all cases, it is infinitely preferable to make the batsman play at the ball rather than leave it alone. Attack all the time, unless the state of the game demands mean, nagging accuracy. It is criminal to waste a new ball by either bowling far too short or letting the batsman leave wide deliveries alone. In such circumstances, you cannot complain if your captain takes you off in favour of someone more reliable, even if he lacks your basic speed or talent. Aim for a well-ordered groove in your bowling, so that you can confidently assess where the next delivery will land. By all means observe the fundamentals of line and length, but have the confidence to try something different once in a while – a fast full-toss, a round-arm slinger, an off-cutter, a slow, swinging yorker. It might just tempt a batsman to a rash stroke, especially if you have tied him down to the extent that he does not know where he can score his runs. A bad ball coming after a series of good deliveries is often the one which gets the wicket in any class of cricket.

If you possess the control and confidence to vary your bowling selectively, you will be a godsend on flat wickets against good batsmen. Some days all you need to do is bowl the style that suits you best – whether fast, swing, seam or cut. They are the good days. On other occasions, the challenge is greater and your captain is looking to you for the breakthrough; it can be achieved by intelligent variation of length, line, position at the bowling crease, or pace at which you let the ball go. Eventually a genuine fast bowler realizes he cannot bowl flat-out all the time and that is when he tries to cross the divide between being a natural, instinctive performer and a thinking cricketer who can still bowl fast on occasions but has learned to appreciate the importance of subtle changes of pace and hand movement. Such a bowler deserves to succeed.

NET PRACTICE

Whatever his standard, no fast bowler can expect to turn up and take a hatful of wickets consistently unless he has worked at his bowling in the nets. The alternative is a slapdash attitude that occasionally yields a good day but more often than not frustration. The fast bowler has to learn where he wants to put the ball at high speed; he cannot do that unless he has practised hard.

When I was at school, cricket was the only thing that held my attention and that point was brought home to me one day as I sat in detention for missing my geography class. The master said to me: 'I've seen you working hard in the nets – why can't you do the same for geography?' There was no answer to that, although I knew even then that I was lucky to be at the kind of school which fostered interest in cricket. Our practice facilities were good, the cricket master was marvellous and there were no excuses for not improving one's own standard. A sad contrast to the current position at many schools in the country. Savage education cutbacks are taking their toll on school cricket – the groundsman is one of the first casualties of the cuts, with the result that the wickets deteriorate and the nets are very poor. If only more money was available, schools could have artificial, all-weather pitches which would mean the ball would not go straight off a length into a boy's mouth and frighten him off cricket for life. Boys would soon come to realize that you dismiss a batsman by skill, rather than terrorising him on a wicket that is positively dangerous.

Practice wickets at any level of the game are now a huge problem. Schoolboys are often scared of a hard cricket ball and the uneven surfaces do nothing to lessen that fear. In club cricket, a fast delivery can behave very erratically against players whose reactions are understandably slow and the quickie gets a false impression of his ability. At county and Test level, the poor wickets in the nets mean the fast bowlers cannot slip themselves because they are worried about injuring the batsmen. In most cases, the run-ups are too short and the footholds too loose, thus a genuine quickie cannot really come roaring in off his usual run-up and has to beware of turning over an ankle in the act of delivery. The England players are supposed to be the best in the country, yet wherever we play in the world, the fast bowlers cannot practise properly against batsmen because of uneven surfaces. It is equally frustrating indoors. The bounce may be even but there is little room for a proper run-up, the result being that the fast bowler lopes in off a John Player League run-up and just ticks over.

Such a situation only serves to confirm my opinion that cricket is basically a batsman's game: the prevailing opinion in the first-class game is that we go along to the nets on behalf of our batsmen, rather than to bowl ourselves back into form. Thus the fast bowler has to do a lot of practice on his own, with no batsman in the net in case he gets injured. I regret to say that this is often an excuse for young bowlers on county staffs to slide away and head for the shower. The prospect of having to think for themselves and work out a consistent bowling line seems to appal many of them and they appear to think that there is no point in practising in the nets unless the coach is on hand to tell them the rights and wrongs. The inherent idleness of young professional cricketers almost amounts to an epidemic. It takes great self-discipline to bowl on your own with just a box of balls for company, while your team-mates are getting changed and relaxing, but the one who stays in the nets will usually be the bowler to progress in the game.

Net practice is important to a fast bowler in one of two ways, depending on his form. If he is going well and everything seems in proper working order, there is no need to go flat out: just run off any stiffness, co-operate with any bats-man who wants to work on his shots and try to widen your own technique. Often a fast bowler stumbles on the fact that he can swing the ball or bowl the off-cutter after he has restricted his run-up in the nets and just ticked over; the pressure is off him, he feels comfortable and can experiment. On the other hand, if the fast bowler is struggling to get full speed and proper rhythm in matches, then some hard work is in store and he must roar in off his full run-up to ensure that he is not guilty of stuttering along, or allowing his head to roll from side to side. It is a case of going back to the basics – is the bowler's head still as he delivers the ball? You would be surprised how many quick bowlers have their eyes almost closed or off-line when they are struggling; they have lapsed into bad habits and do not realize that after a long spell in the nets. It is no use believing that the bowling action alone will get back the accuracy and speed through the air: look where you want to pitch the ball and keep the head perfectly still at the moment of delivery.

The essence of net practice is realizing that you have to practise something at far greater length than you will ever need for a match. A fast bowler might deliver a yorker once every five overs during a game: he must practise it for half an hour. The same applies to the bouncer and all the variations of swing and cut. Always remember that you are in the nets for a purpose – avoid fooling around with your mates and concentrate on the ball about to be delivered rather than the next quip. Get fully limbered up beforehand, going through your stretching and bending routines. Have a clearly defined plan for that session: you might be worried about your run-up or that you are not bowling very successfully from round the wicket. If you think you are bowling too many no-balls, ask a colleague to watch you in your run-up and try to get someone standing up to the stumps as umpire – some bowlers occasionally get disconcerted by the physical presence of an umpire when they are plagued by no-ball trouble. Practise bowling in overs: tell yourself that the fourth ball is going to be a yorker, followed by two outswingers. Check out your follow-through, something you cannot achieve satisfactorily when you are hemmed in by another net. Ask other bowlers to check you out in net practice and do the same for them. Never take your technique for granted, as it is easy to slip into careless habits that will be spotted by others if they will only take the time to help.

When bowling at a batsman in the nets, I would advise keeping the ball well up – partly because of the uneven surface and also because you get into the proper habit of allowing the ball to swing late. If you do want to practise bowling bouncers, do it against one of the best batsmen and always let him know that one is on its way; there is nothing funny or clever about laying out one of your team-mates with a delivery that splits his head. Ideally, bouncers should be tried in an empty net before a batsman gets involved. Wherever possible, the fast bowler should work in harness with a batsman; if he wants to work at a particular stroke to a specific delivery, it is good practice for the bowler to concentrate on his accuracy.

An empty net should be used for the fastest bowling. The traditional method of bowling in an empty net – a box of balls and one stump – is still the best for me. Insert the stump in the hole for the off stump, because that should be your usual line. Alec Bedser used to place a white handkerchief on the spot for an ideal 'length-and-line' delivery, and he would practise hitting that for hours. Keep your eyes glued on the target as you run in: lack of accuracy can often be traced to taking the eyes off the marker or the base of the stumps. The same discipline applies for the yorker, except that the ball must be pitched that little bit further up to the stumps.

Sometimes life can get a little lonely in an empty net for the fast bowler, but if he is lucky he can rope in some other bowlers to vary the training. Introduce an element of competition by getting everyone to aim for the same spot. If you hit the stump, that is three points to the bowler: tally up the scores after 30 minutes and see who comes out on top. If it is not you, then try to be the best next time around. Vary the competition, again for half an hour, by bowling six balls in a row off your proper run, trying to hit a small target placed on a good length on the line of the off stump: one point for hitting the target and another for hitting the stump. Then place a cricket ball on the target, an even more difficult task – four points if you hit it. The same sort of practice could be used for the yorker by placing the target on the popping crease in front of the stumps.

You will be lucky if you can manage such competitions regularly because they ease the boredom of slogging away on your own. The less fortunate fast bowlers have to view such diversions as a bonus and get on with the unrelenting task of bowling hour after hour in the nets. The goal is being able to bowl a specific delivery at any stage in a match and the satisfaction that results is worth all the hard work.

4
MENTAL FITNESS

The area of mental fitness is a shadowy one, but nevertheless vital for anyone who wishes to make it to the top as a fast bowler. Further down the scale of ambition, I believe schoolboys and club cricketers can all benefit if they organize their minds. I hasten to add that I am not suggesting making a game more serious when it is being played primarily for fun – simply that thinking clearly and positively at the right times can make you a better fast bowler.

The ideal mental qualities are many and varied: pride, the desire to set and maintain a high standard of performance; resilience to set-backs and guts to get through the pain barrier; optimism – the conviction that you are going to get wickets and have a decisive say in the game; an unflappability over dropped catches and snicks to the boundary; the commitment that means you always want to bowl, no matter the conditions or state of the wicket; flexibility – being able to alter strategy; the perception to spot a batsman's weakness and capitalize on it; a steely attitude towards making life hard for the batsman; the intelligence to listen to advice and apply it where appropriate; the self-discipline to forget poor deliveries and refrain from histrionics and bad behaviour on the field; a powerful enough ego to relish challenges with the best batsmen. No fast bowler in history has ever had a perfect combination of all these qualities, and I am no exception. When things are going wrong, I have to steel myself against succumbing to the pessimistic streak in my nature. I have a slight inferiority complex about my technical deficiencies and sometimes tend to place other fast bowlers on a pedestal at my expense. However, I believe I am fairly strong in most of these departments – working hard at keying myself up for the day's action, refusing to get sidetracked by things that go against me on the field and just knuckling down to get the job done. For me, fast bowling is difficult enough at the best of times, so why makes things worse through defects of temperament?

I did not become mentally strong for cricket until I had been in the first-class game for almost ten years. I was never relaxed enough to be confident that I could dredge up a performance to win a Test; many other fast bowlers seemed much more talented practitioners than me and I would readily make excuses for myself. A chance conversation in Australia changed my attitude: I turned to hypnotism. Dr Arthur Jackson was an old friend of mine and he had noticed how tense and jumpy I had become, to the detriment of my efforts on the field. As a qualified hypnotherapist, Arthur knew the value of a settled, contented mind and he gave me a session. A single 20-minute spell on his couch changed me and made me a better fast bowler: he helped clear my mind, assess my defects and my assets as a cricketer and guided me towards a coherent programme of rehabilitation. I embarked on a comprehensive physical training programme which improved my stamina and fitness to a remarkable degree; I became England's premier fast bowler and the doubts eased. I still have trouble with insomnia during the season and I sometimes get too keyed up – but Arthur Jackson's tapes often help me see things in perspective.

Many people have said to me that I look in a dream world when bowling in a match. Certainly I hardly recognize myself when I see the highlights on television and watch my glazed eyes and set expression. Well that is simply the way I am when working. I need to concentrate on the delicate mechanism of fast bowling and cannot allow myself the luxuries of social chit-chat. By nature, I am a fairly unexcitable, unflappable person and I do not see why you have to be demonstrative to be firmly committed. I need to have everything right in my mind. The hypnotherapy sessions have been invaluable in this respect, but I would not recommend them to anyone unless it was expedient.

Hypnotherapy came at just the right time in my career but fortunately there are not many who approach the game of cricket with my kind of single-minded intensity. I find the pressures of top-class cricket very hard: after a long day in the field, I do not want to talk about the game and just want to get away from the ground, have a bite to eat and get to bed early. I am usually physically and mentally drained from the effort of bowling and normally cannot perform at my best for at least another 24 hours. My colleagues who can relax boisterously, enjoy a few beers and look forward to the next day have my admiration and envy. I have to think through the day's play and work out things for the rest of the game. Of course I take it too seriously but there is nothing I can do about that at this stage in my career, other than to advise all other cricketers to enjoy themselves. Club players should try their hardest during the game without losing sight of a sense of enjoyment, and then switch off at stumps – the clubhouse should be like the nineteenth hole in golf. As for schoolboys – just go out and have fun, lads.

In my own idiosyncratic way, I do enjoy most of the pressures associated with fast bowling, even though I have a funny way of demonstrating the fact. I relish the sensation of feeling fit, of knowing that I can keep going when others might be struggling around me. The responsibility of being the main strike bowler suits me, it instils a sense of purpose. The last 15 minutes before I go out on to the field to bowl are always engrossing. Normally I will know who the opposition's opening batsmen are and I will have worked out where I am going to bowl at them. I will have a reasonable knowledge of how the wicket is going to play and what kind of field I shall employ. The nerve-ends will be jangling a little, but consolation is at hand with the realization that any top-class sportsman who does not feel a little nervous at such a stage has lost the appetite for the task. After all, the batsmen must be equally tense: all I have to do is simply send the ball down to them and see what they can do with it. The more extrovert members of my side will be walking around the dressing-room, playing pranks on others, singing or cracking jokes – that is just a cloak for their nerves. I am content to sit quietly, psyching myself, 'it's going to be your day, you are going to make your own luck by willpower.'

That is the easy part. Putting those admirable sentiments into practice a few minutes later is the real test. I like to think through an over, chastising myself as I walk back to my mark or trying to remember everything about the particular batsman's weakness. It is a case of tunnel vision for me when I start an over. I can do without conferences and field changes if the same batsman remains on strike. I tune myself into my job, do it to the best of my ability and think very hard indeed. I could never approach the task in the way of Dennis Lillee. When he walks through the gate on to the pitch it is akin to stepping on to the stage for him. He loves the sense of theatre and seems to bowl better as he goes through his routine of histrionics. Lillee loves to play the melodramatic villain while I happily settle for the back end of the horse if I can do my job properly. I want to exert my authority over the proceedings but in a cold, implacable way; the batsmen must feel I am never going to give them respite, that I shall remain at their throats. I force myself to look fresh and positive, even though my aching feet and pounding chest intimate otherwise. I keep telling myself that I need only one mistake from the batsman and he is mine.

Try not to be distracted by events out of your control, particularly dropped catches which can be an endless source of frustration for a fast bowler. You get everything right in your approach to the wicket, bowl one that little bit quicker and shorter which disconcerts the batsman, who fends the ball off to a close fielder. He then drops it. Your colleagues murmur 'bad luck', the batsman looks sheepish and pleased at the same time and you are left standing in the middle of the wicket, feeling flat and empty. Console yourself with the fact that you did your best, that you have no control over the seemingly easy act of cupping the hands round a ball that is falling gently to earth. You can do nothing about a delivery as soon as the ball has left your hand. Turn round, get back to your mark and try again. Now I appreciate that is asking a lot of any fast bowler, whether he is on the village green, in a school match or playing for his country; I too used to make a song and dance about a missed catch until I realized that getting distracted from the task meant the batsman was doubly fortunate. Nobody drops a catch on purpose and the fielder feels far worse than the bowler.

The same philosophical attitude should apply to misfields and snicks to the boundary. If the ball is being slogged or edged near a fielder, then at least you are bowling to your field and with luck things will turn your way soon. However, if you are being played into wide open spaces that is bad bowling, even if the ball is in the air and the stroke is fortuitous. Look to your own defects, rather than those of your colleagues. When someone turns a single into a boundary off your bowling, remember that you are no gazelle yourself, that brilliant fielders have saved many runs for you in the past and that wonderful catches have often been taken to give you undeserved wickets.

If you are lucky enough to play the kind of cricket where batsmen 'walk' when they know they are out, never forget to thank them as they head for the pavilion – such people are becoming rarer, I am afraid. Hardly anybody does that nowadays in first-class cricket, a situation that I deplore. In such circumstances you simply have to shut your mind off from being robbed of a wicket. If you allow yourself to be drawn into a slanging match, or brood about the decision, you will not bowl as well as before the incident.

I really have no time for those who indulge in histrionics or verbal intimidation on the cricket field. For me it has no place in the game at any level and Test cricketers have a particular responsibility to stamp it out. Youngsters who watch us on television are aping the customs of the more boorish Test cricketers and you can see the results on the village green and in school matches. The captain and umpires should not hesitate to have strong words with anyone who misbehaves on the field. Fast bowlers are more susceptible than most to the temptation to indulge in 'verbals'; they are wound up to a peak of commitment, with their nerves on edge and temperamental explosions are never far from the surface. Yet a fast bowler who loses his temper ends up bowling badly, even if he has psyched himself up properly. How can he possibly think through his bowling strategy when he is yapping away at the batsman and being insolent to the umpire? Everybody wants to win the game and play a decisive part in it, but the real essence of cricket at any level is to play as hard and as fairly as you can without behaving like a prima-donna.

Umpiring decisions go against the bowler during almost every bowling spell, so there is no point in getting despondent over them, let alone resorting to histrionics. Standing incredulous with hands on hips demeans you and the game. I appreciate that club and school cricket is full of umpires whose interpretation of the laws can be suspect, but at least they have given up their time to supervize a pastime in which you have the chance to enjoy yourself among pleasant company. I find it incredible that some club players take umpires' decisions so badly; it seems to spill over from league cricket, where points are so vital for league positions, and from the first-class game, where sportsmanship is on the wane. The best way to deal with an umpire who you know has made a bad decision off your bowling is to help him. Why should he have to give reasons for his decision? An umpire should not have to justify himself in any class of cricket. Just accept his ruling and get on with your bowling. The more you criticise him, the less likely he will be to give you a favourable verdict next time you appeal.

It is equally hard to be detached when you are being smashed about the field and your morale is declining as a result. It can be fairly humiliating to run into someone like Viv Richards when he is seeing the ball so well that you know you are going to be taken apart with contempt. Such days normally coincide with no-ball problems, or some unspecified psychological malaise that impairs your rhythm, control and confidence. The great players seem to sense that and you suffer accordingly. When a fast bowler is going well, the over seems to rush past: I have often been staggered when the umpire calls 'over', when I could have sworn I had at least one delivery to go. On the other hand, a fast bowler who is out of sorts knows exactly how many balls are left. That is the time when you think, 'Please get me through this over without a no-ball. I just want to survive the next couple of balls and think it through. I'll be all right if he doesn't hammer me in this over.' You just have to clench your teeth, pray for an easy approach to the crease and tell yourself, 'Right, just two balls left – make 'em good ones. Nothing wrong with "dot" balls.' When bowling against a great batsman who has the bit between the teeth, I have often aimed no higher than a maiden over and judged it an achievement. Then you just have to hope that he will fret at being tied down for an over and take chances subsequently. Sometimes, a fast bowler simply has to try to survive and leave the joining of battle to later on.

All fast bowlers hate being hit to the boundary, especially by an authentic stroke from a batsman who seems well in command. If he strokes the quickie through the covers, you can almost be sure that the next delivery will be a bouncer, or at least a hostile, short-pitched delivery. The bowler's pride has been stung and he reacts aggressively and quite within his rights. That is all very well, but anger should only last for one ball. He must regain his calm and continue thinking clearly otherwise his bowling suffers and he will spray the ball all over the place. In my early days in the England side, Derek Underwood was invaluable at calming me down after I had been smashed to the boundary. He would collect the ball, walk back with me from mid-on, telling me to relax while I would shout: 'Give me that . . . ball!' He taught me to avoid getting caught up in the emotion of the moment, to clear the 'red mists' and start again. All bowlers should work at hiding their displeasure from the batsman and get back to the start of their run-up with no fuss. At moments like this, Dennis Lillee shows his greatness: he gives that characteristic flick of sweat from the brow with one finger, then stalks back without any stage-managed theatricals . . . and then replies in the grand manner.

Such detachment is needed when a fast bowler has injured a batsman. Let me underline that at club or school level a fast bowler should not go out to hurt anyone. The batsmen lack proper protection, the wickets are unreliable and the fast bowler should be aiming at the stumps, not the body, for most of the time. It is a different matter, however, in first-class cricket. The days of helmets and padding were long overdue and their introduction allowed fast bowlers to indulge in legitimate, short-pitched deliveries. Strong umpiring is needed to curb any excesses in the amount of intimidation, but as a general principle I see no harm in a fast bowler striving to ruffle or even frighten a batsman wearing the necessary protective clothing. I have never gone out of my way to injure a batsman, but when this has unfortunately happened I have steeled myself from getting too upset at the sight of blood or a broken bone. There is the element of the bullfight about a contest between fast bowler and batsman and while I am no supporter of the hard-faced 'win-at-all-costs' school, I will bowl a similar delivery if the batsman has been frightened or hurt by me. Within the rules of the game, you have to be relentless, uncompromising and occasionally ruthless.

Stereotypes abound in all sports and the one attached to the fast bowler lingers. He is supposed to be large, mean, fond of beer during the intervals and simply concerned with bowling as fast as possible without subtlety. In my experience, fast bowlers think as deeply about their craft as any other cricketers: I pride myself on my memory of batsmen's weaknesses, how I have dismissed them in the past, what their best shots are and where they can be tied down. We may not indulge in 'spider-and-the-fly' tactics in the same way as a slow bowler, but we have a good idea what we should be bowling at most stages. The same thing should apply to fast bowlers of any standard – you may not be able to land the ball on the precise spot, but you should have the ability to 'think out' a batsman.

If you spot a weakness, set an attacking field and hammer away at the flaw. It could be anything: a tendency to drive uppishly, an instinctive habit of stepping away towards leg for the defensive shot, a weakness for hooking in the air. Watch out for the signs and adjust accordingly. The same applies to his strengths. If he likes to play off the back foot, then post a gully and third man for the cut and pitch the ball well up to him. Get him fretting, wondering where he can score his runs. Keep your eyes open when resting between spells: you might spot that a batsman shapes to play on the off side, so think about bowling on his legs. If he favours the leg side, you could try going round the wicket, angling the ball across his body and hoping for a catch in the slips. Avoid being mentally lazy, even when bowling hard after a good long spell.

It is easy to have mental blocks about some types of batsmen. Left-handers have caused me more trouble than I would have liked during my career. Early on, I did little with the ball other than hurl it down fast; when bowling at a left-hander, I would come wide of the crease and try to slant it across the body, but they soon worked that one out. Eventually, I learned to vary my pace a little and use the crease more intelligently but I still find it hard against left-handers. I have to pitch the ball about 18 inches from the right-hander's line and also concentrate on keeping off the wicket in my follow-through. Left-handers tend to shield most of the stumps and it is disconcerting to see only a batsman's body as you run in – it is like shooting at a moving target. I wish I had experimented more at bowling round the wicket, which serves two purposes in that it gives you a better sight of the stumps and presents the left-hander with a different angle of flight. An opening pair containing one left-hander can be a fast bowler's nightmare because you have to concentrate hard at bowling a different line, while maintaining your speed. They really can mess you up and if the quick bowler is trying to sort out his area of attack, the batsmen are already on top.

One of the biggest psychological strains on a fast bowler comes when he starts bowling 'no-balls' in a match. You cannot go off to the sanctuary of a net to work out the problem calmly and sensibly: your job is to break through the batting order, not be a passenger. It invariably seems to strike when good batsmen are at the crease, players who will gladly take advantage of the free hit that comes from a no-ball. The over looks as if it will never end and the alternative is a succession of pallid, medium-pace deliveries that would not trouble your mother. You start to feel fatigued and the captain looks anxiously at you far too often for peace of mind. All I can suggest is to run straighter, get nearer to the stumps, avoid looking down at your feet and battle through. It is something that I have learned to live with over the years. With a run-up like a snake, I will always run the risk of over-stepping after steaming in for 35 yards. When it feels right, I give an instinctive little nod as my left foot hits the mark signifying that start of my sprint. Most fast bowlers who regularly strive for extra effort in their delivery know that on some days they will be out of step. They must react to the cry of 'no-ball' phlegmatically and concentrate grimly on eradicating the fault, rather than getting at the umpire.

Solid, sensible advice is often invaluable when no-ball trouble looms, but there is a danger that the mind can get too cluttered with well-meaning words from too many sources. When things go wrong, I tend to turn to as few people as possible and then sift through the advice I am given. I have seen many promising fast bowlers ruined by taking in every scrap of confusing guidance and feel it is always best to tackle the problem clear-sightedly. I tell myself that there cannot be anything radically wrong if I am bowling in the same way that has been good enough for England for more than a decade and that a little tinkering here and there is sufficient. I do not mean to sound arrogant on this point, but wish to emphasize that panic-stricken surgery on a drastic scale can ruin the fast bowler's action, control and confidence. The club bowler should seek out someone whose opinion and honesty he respects, not a colleague who may be jealous of his ability to bowl fast. Ask for some plain, straight talking without technical jargon. The fault could be something slight, such as an undue emphasis on pace in part of the run-up, or an over-reliance on line and length while sacrificing speed. Whatever the diagnosis, think about it and go and work it out in the nets. Psychological crises should not happen out in the middle.

The fast bowler must always think about structuring his over to suit the particular state of the game. At the start of the innings, most of us are happy just to drop the ball in a respectable area before letting ourselves slip; at other times, all-out attack is vital to get a breakthrough. You may be required to keep a good player on strike throughout your over so that the inferior batsman will have to cope with the wiles of a slow bowler during the next over. When that happens you will have to sacrifice a little speed in the interest of bowling tightly to stop him getting away from you. Conversely, your bowling partner has done his bit by bottling up the good player and leaving the tailender to the mercy of your pace and hostility – your job then is to dismiss him without delay. Do not waste a single delivery, make him play all the time; if he can play forward with comfort, dig the ball in at his ribs and get him fishing at the chest-high delivery that is leaving him. When the tactics dictate, vary your attack with a yorker, a slower ball or even come round the wicket. Always remember there are times to experiment and other occasions when you have to lower your sights for the good of the team. Be alive to the shifting circumstances during an innings.

Pitting your skills and tactical acumen against good players should bring out the best in a fast bowler. The better the batsman, the better you should bowl: rise to the occasion, rather than expect the worst to happen. In effect it is a clash of egos – the good batsman feels he can take you apart and you are willing yourself to come out on top. Confidence in your ability – channelled in the proper, sensible direction – is a necessary adjunct to pride in your own performance.

The young fast bowler with the right positive attitude will be the one who progresses in the game, instead of the talented one who feels the opposition batsmen are too strong. When I came into first-class cricket, I would make all sorts of excuses for myself. My stock response was, 'Oh, the wicket's too slow, you can't expect a fast bowler to do anything on that.' Subconsciously, I was stepping aside on behalf of others whom I thought had greater ability; my attitude was just a cover for a sense of inferiority. My attitude to the pain barrier was also passive. When the going was tough, I would throw the towel in because I lacked the inner confidence that stems from superior fitness. Injury after injury dogged me and it seemed as if I would never get my mind attuned to consistently hostile fast bowling. I am sure that most cricketers believe that fast bowlers are hypochondriacs, because we always seem to be worried about some physical problem. That stems from the effort involved in bowling fast, yet I do feel that unless you are properly fit your thought processes cannot be satisfactorily channelled in the right direction. A fast bowler dogged by fears that he could break down any over is in no psychological state to triumph over batsmen.

You need a resilient, determined streak in your nature that makes you keep going and stills the nagging doubts. The ability to battle through against adversity and triumph by sheer willpower is something that comes with experience. It helped me attain my most spectacular performance in my Test career when, to all intents and purposes, I was on the way out. The Leeds Test of 1981 will be remembered as one of the great England–Australia contests, and my part in taking 8 for 43 to clinch victory by 18 runs has been well chronicled. I remember it as the biggest crisis of my career. Because of a flu bug, I had not bowled terribly well in the previous Test at Lord's and was not originally selected for Leeds. Alec Bedser, the chairman of selectors, rang me to break the news and I somehow talked my way back into the squad by convincing him I was fit enough after a bad cold. I did not take any wickets in the first innings on a pitch that was helpful to me and I knew that I would have to pull out something special from the bag in the second innings. Thanks to the brilliance of Ian Botham, we managed to scrape together enough runs to set at least some sort of target – 130 to be precise.

The fact that Mike Brearley did not choose me to open the bowling – indeed I was the fourth bowler to be used – brought home to me that he no longer saw me as his match winner. My pride was hurt, and with Australia 56 for one it looked as if we were all going to be downcast within a couple of hours. I told Brearley I could not bowl satisfactorily uphill and into the wind and pleaded for a shot at the other end. I got my way and soon wickets started to fall on a pitch that was getting more and more unreliable. I picked up wickets with short-of-a-length bowling aimed for cracks in the pitch and the Australians began to panic. Then Ray Bright and Dennis Lillee started to play sensibly, Lillee scoring off the short stuff and Bright getting out of the way. I decided to change my tactics and pitch the ball up to them. It worked when Lillee tried to drive and Mike Gatting took a marvellous tumbling catch at wide mid-on. With the last pair together and just a handful of runs needed, I had to work out how to bowl at Bright; having got this close, I was desperate to see us win. I decided to pitch the ball up and take a chance on him driving me away through open spaces. I prayed to deliver a fast yorker and it came along: Bright clean-bowled, Australia all out 111. A fantastic feeling, of course, but what pleased me most of all was that I had shown tactical flexibility in altering my line of attack to Bright and Lillee after succeeding earlier with bowling a little short. I was really psyched up, knowing that my future with England was on the line that afternoon. I have always believed that a couple of mediocre games spells danger for a Test fast bowler in his thirties and Leeds 1981 would have been my last Test if I had not gritted my teeth and reacted positively to the pressure. It was one of those days when I knew I just had to make things happen and all the experience I had gained over the years got me through.

Of course, that performance merely postponed the day of judgement. It is terribly difficult to be clear-minded about the effects of age and pressure on any fast bowler in any class of cricket. As you get older, you tend to know your capabilities and develop a certain amount of cunning, but there is no avoiding the fact that a fast bowler basically relies on speed. If it is no longer there, his days are numbered. He has to be honest with himself and assess whether the decline in form is temporary and can be cured in the nets, or if his cutting edge has been blunted for good. If he is lucky enough, he will have picked up enough technical know-how to get him through an innings at medium pace. In my case, injury and a consequent lack of fitness will determine how long I carry on as a fast bowler. Having worked so hard over recent years to sort out my bowling style, I would have thought I could keep going as long as my fitness lasts. Another serious injury would set me back, however, and the question will then be whether I could possibly recover an acceptable level of fitness to regain my speed. If not, I shall have to practice hard at those off-cutters!

So I am no different from the humblest trundler on the village green who does not know how long he can keep going. I can be certain about one thing, however: all the technical expertise and physical excellence a fast bowler can muster is of little consequence unless he knows what to do with it all. Brains must be allied to brawn; the attitude must be as right as the grip for the out-swinger. I wish I had grasped that principle a lot earlier in my career.

5
PHYSICAL FITNESS

A fast bowler has to be fitter than anyone else in the team. The component parts of his body are put under great strain and inevitably he sometimes breaks down or fails to perform at his best due to fatigue. If he is fit, he is automatically a better bowler: it will take longer to get tired and his concentration will not be impaired by the distractions of tiredness. Natural ability will get you only so far but the most mediocre fast bowler can improve his overall standard if he learns to take better care of himself. The game is not played just in the first hour, when you are fresh enough to come roaring in off a long run and make the batsmen hop about: late in the innings, you are supposed to get stuck in with a ragged old ball in your hand and the pace gone from the wicket. Then is the time you need to be able to concentrate on delivering the next ball, rather than worrying about your sore shoulder or heaving chest; the aim is to give of your best in a hostile, fast spell at any stage of the game.

In club cricket there is so much scope for a fast bowler who keeps himself fit. Most opening bowlers are finished after their first spell – say, after eight overs – and they stiffen up in the field afterwards and cannot fire on all cylinders when the captain brings them back for another blast. Yet if you can earn yourself a reputation for stamina and reliability you will be recognized as a potential matchwinner, irrespective of your inability to bowl the outswinger or yorker. This is not so important in school cricket, where the games are shorter and the boys are rightly going out to enjoy themselves, but, as they get older, they should be made to realize that fitness is an essential part of becoming a better cricketer. It also helps prolong a career: most cricketers hate the idea of packing up because they are too old. The man who used to be a fearsome quickie is now a slow-medium trundler, his arm getting lower and lower as the season wears on; he tells himself he can still keep his end up as a bowler but it is the fielding that exposes him. I find that sad, especially if the veteran is still crazy about the game, because the remedy for prolonging his participation has always been in his hands – all that is needed is guts and application on a sensible scale.

To be fit for fast bowling you need to train properly in four separate areas to build up stamina, muscle mobility and strength. Your most vulnerable areas are the groin, hamstring, back and legs and an organized training programme will

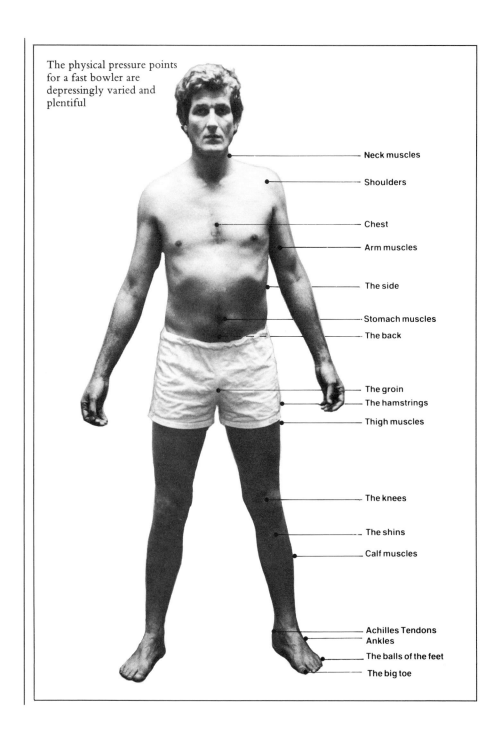

The physical pressure points for a fast bowler are depressingly varied and plentiful

Neck muscles

Shoulders

Chest

Arm muscles

The side

Stomach muscles

The back

The groin

The hamstrings

Thigh muscles

The knees

The shins

Calf muscles

Achilles Tendons

Ankles

The balls of the feet

The big toe

cater for all those. You have to live with minor pains – aching feet, sore toes, a weak ankle – and raise your pain threshold. Tell yourself you can live with the niggles, that you must get to the end of the over. Getting used to pain is something novel to many club cricketers, but if they have got stuck into training they will be used to the feeling and know how to cope with it. Fast bowling at any level is literally a survival of the fittest: you get out of it what you put into it. If you do not find your training hard work, then you are not training properly and you will lack reserves of stamina just when you need them. There is no point in cheating.

A fast bowler is really fit only at the start of the season. After a few games, the physical strain takes its toll and you have to battle through. You may have to spring up to the bowling crease about 150 times in a day, as well as wrench your body through your delivery stride. You have to be strong, of course, but not muscle-bound, which would make you stiffen up after the first spell. There must be a happy medium between strength and stamina – many great fast bowlers may not have been tall and well-developed, but they could make their physical resources last all day without affecting their bowling. Whatever your physique, you should work hard at getting the best out of it.

My physique is hardly impressive, apart from my height. In my early days in first-class cricket I often broke down under the strain of bowling fast for long spells. I was lazy, looking for any excuse to skip training: I wanted to get fit but did not want to work too hard at it in case I broke down again. When I recovered from injury, I may have been fit to play cricket, but not to bowl consistently fast. This mental block about fitness meant I was drifting through my career with no real hope of great advancement. At this stage international rivals like Dennis Lillee were at least four times as fit as me. In the final period of a day's play I would be whacked, cannon fodder for a good batsman. Dr Arthur Jackson's honest, direct words changed all that. His hypnosis helped to sort out my muddled approach to cricket while relaxing me and his advice on training opened up new worlds to me. He gave me a book by the German athletics coach Ernst Van Aaken, outlining his training methods. My initial involvement with his methods coincided with my first injury-free season and I have not looked back since.

There is no hidden secret about the ways I keep fit to bowl fast at the top level. Anybody of any age can do it at little cost. Basically it involves running, sprinting and strength and stretching exercises. Running long distances builds up stamina, the sprinting develops explosiveness in the delivery stride and sharpens your run-up, and the stretching exercises ward off aches and pains and torn muscles. None of these routines takes up too much time. You should do some sort of training every day – as you get older it becomes even more vital. A fast bowler over

30 is weaker, has less stamina, less muscle-flexibility and his reactions are slower. Injuries take longer to clear up and his arms get lower and lower. He compensates for the physical decline with a shrewder awareness of the technique of fast bowling, but nevertheless he must work very hard to maintain a general level of fitness. Let us take a detailed look at the methods I use to keep fit for bowling.

STRENGTH TRAINING

I do this in a local gymnasium. There are similar ones in every city in the country but do not worry if you are nowhere near one: many of the exercises I shall cover can be done at home. I would not recommend them for someone under the age of 16 – he has plenty of time before gruesome things like pain barriers dog him, so let us leave him to enjoy his cricket for the time being.

Basically, the gym work is circuit-training. It has been worked out by a qualified physical-training expert and the idea is to develop all parts of the body without turning you into someone with Mr Universe biceps. The parts of the circuit that you find most painful are the ones on which you should concentrate – your vulnerable areas have been discovered.

An ideal way to warm up before attempting the circuit: five minutes on the bike, with the gears being adjusted accordingly to make it tougher as the weeks go by.

(1) Sit-ups Lie back with your legs at an angle to a bar. With your hands behind your neck, bring your head forward to touch your knees. Start off in groups of ten with the bar at a reasonable angle. As you get fitter, the bar will be tilted upwards. You should do about 70 sit-ups in a circuit – seven sets of ten. interspersed with the other exercises. They are vital for stomach muscles, the area that takes a lot of strain when you are delivering the ball. Having strained my stomach muscles twice, I can confirm how painful it can be and how important sit-ups are, despite the pain. They can be done at home, provided you anchor your feet.

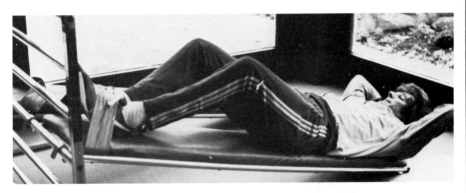

(2) Arm-pulls From a standing position, pull a 50-lbs weight from above your head down to your knees. Start off doing it 15 times and graduate to 25, with a 70-lbs weight. A good exercise for arm muscles, the chest and thighs.

(3) Neck-presses Sit down on a bench and pull a 40-lbs weight from above the head to the back of the neck. Start off with 15 going up to 25, with a 60-lbs weight. This strengthens up the neck, arms and shoulder muscles.

(4) Pectoral exercises Lie back on a bench and with 5-lbs weights in each hand bring them together: three lots of tens and eventually four lots of twelves. A good one to broaden and deepen the chest.

(5) Leg machine Sit upright and pull a weighted bar of about 15 lbs through a 90-degree angle: three lots of tens rising to four lots of twelves. This builds up the muscles at the bottom of the front thigh, which act as a cushion for the pounding the knee joint receives in running to the wicket and delivering the ball.

(6) Hamstring exercises Lie on a board at an angle of 45 degrees and press a 10-lbs bar three times back over your head. Take it down to your feet, with the knees locked, and stretch forward three times. Do that between 15 and 25 times. Take your time, give it a good slow stretch. Hamstrings are very important to a fast bowler and must be long and strong; if they tear, you face a long and painful time out of the game.

(7) Back extensions Stay on the same board for the hamstring exercise and turn yourself round. With hands gripped behind the back, lift up the front of your torso as far as possible and hold it there for five seconds. Do that 15 times and aim for 25 eventually. To make it even more arduous, hold a 20-lbs weight on the back of your neck while stretching back.

(8) Bench-presses With my poorly developed arm muscles, I dread this one. Lie back on a bench with a 20-lbs weight and lift it up and down as much as possible. End up with a 60-lbs weight and 40 lifts. Repetition is more important than lifting a very heavy one just a few times: you need to get the chest and arm muscles working hard, but not so you look like Mr Universe. Also good exercise to regulate breathing.

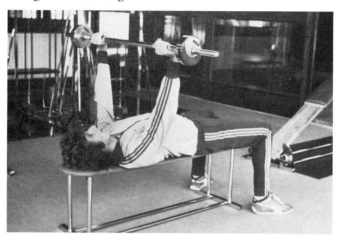

(9) Half-squats Use the same weight as for the bench presses and sit upright on the bench, with the weight behind your neck. Stand up and sit down, with your knees locked, back straight and head erect. Very good for the hips and thighs. Aim for 40 squats with a 60-lbs weight.

(10) Step-ups With a 20-lbs weight in either hand, step up and down from a bench. Left foot first 15 times, then change to the right foot for the same number. Try to get up to 25 times. This one really gets the heartbeat going and is ideal for the trunk, hamstring, arm and calf muscles. A boxer's exercise, this one, and reminiscent of the way footballers used to train by running up and down the terraces.

(11) Leg machine Back to the leg machine, but this time lie face down with no weights involved. Put your legs under the bar, bend the knees and bring the bar back to near your bottom. Guide it back down again. Start off with three lots of tens, ending up with four lots of twelves. A good exercise for the hamstrings.

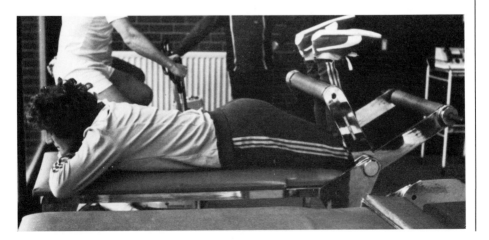

(12) Power jogging This is done on a running machine with gradients that can be altered depending on your fitness. Just a couple of minutes initially, then anything up to 15 minutes. Push yourself hard – it is the last exercise in the circuit – and get up a good sweat. After that, check your pulse rate and relax. If your recovery rate improves on every visit, then you are getting fitter. If you are managing to breathe fairly easily, do a few more exercises.

Do not worry about collapsing and being carried off to hospital in a coma. All these gymnasia are staffed by qualified trainers who keep an eye on you, check out your heartbeat at regular intervals and give you the right sort of encouragement. Tell them how unfit you really think you are, detail any injuries or long-standing physical defects and they will take care of you. Remember to intersperse the exercises with those dreaded sit-ups which are marvellous for the stomach muscles and the beer belly.

I do this gym work in the spring and autumn, but there is no reason why a club cricketer cannot get to one at least once a week if it is within reasonable distance. The feeling of fitness is well worth the few pounds it costs. There is a great sense of achievement in mastering the difficult task of disciplining yourself to hammer your body. There is no point in dipping out on some of the exercises because you are only cheating yourself. After the first session, you will feel stiff and sore for a couple of days. The temptation is to say, 'Oh, that doesn't suit me because I feel terrible,' but if you stick with it there will come a time when you are not stiff the following day and simply pleasantly tired that night. Freeze the mind when you walk in that gym: you are paying for it, so make sure you get your money's worth. Store up a few things to think about when doing the exercises; take your time and do not snatch at anything. When you get that terrible tightness across the chest or in the muscles, just lie back for a moment. You will think you cannot possibly do another sit-up or lift another weight, but if you relax a little, breathe in some oxygen, the batteries will be recharged shortly. There is a fine dividing line between masochism and doing yourself justice in training, but you have to discover what your pain threshold is, to know if you can call on your reserves of energy when bowling.

Be careful with weight training. It is, of course, important for a fast bowler to build his biceps but bad injuries can be picked up by aiming too high with weights. Ask to be supervized and never lose sight of the fact that a fast bowler needs to be supple and flexible, rather than massively muscular.

RUNNING PROGRAMME

I have never felt so well since I began running every day. My stamina has increased dramatically, thanks to the strengthening of my heart and lungs. It has disciplined my breathing, so that I take in air at the right time as I walk back to the mark, thereby calming me down. When I was struggling to come to terms with the physical demands of fast bowling, Dennis Lillee told me that distance-running had helped him more than anything else – how right he was.

Anyone can do it and be a better bowler as a result. All you have to do is sacrifice three-quarters of an hour every day. Get out of bed earlier, or do it before dinner after getting home from work. Do it religiously every day throughout the year. Only black ice or snow should hold you back – I find the rain very refreshing on a run. Get yourself some decent footwear – soft, pliable running-shoes with firm padding in the vulnerable areas of the foot – and a tracksuit, and you are ready.

The first day is the worst. Grit your teeth and run at a speed slow enough to enable you, if necessary, to hold a conversation. Try to keep going for a quarter of an hour. The following day will find you stiff and miserable but it is imperative to force yourself back into your tracksuit. Increase your run by five minutes on the third day and aim to finish the first week with a half-hour effort.

In the second week, step up your pace and start timing yourself. Try to run further in 30 minutes, or the original distance in as short a time as possible. You should be able to manage three miles in 30 minutes, leading on to five miles in 35 minutes. Prepare your mind for what is basically a boring pursuit. If you have a problem, save it for the daily run and try to work it out while plodding along. Find a pleasant spot for the task and do not get carried away with speed – remember, distance-running is for stamina. Always have a hot bath or shower and change of clothing within a couple of minutes of finishing your run. You will, I promise, feel terrific once you get into the habit; a hearty breakfast tastes marvellous after mortifying the flesh while everyone else is snoring or lolling around.

Before the season starts I do a lot of running to build up my powers of endurance. Every day I run three miles against the clock, aiming for a time of about 19 minutes. Once a week I will really push myself: five miles at under 35 minutes and, later, one mile at about six minutes. During the season I run three miles when I am not playing or certain not to bowl, but if I know that I shall be bowling, then I conserve my energy. Before nets I aim for ten minutes lapping the ground, just to get the pulse stirring and rid of the cobwebs.

The sight of cricketers running often leads to muttering and head-shaking among the older brigade of diehards. During the first season in which I used a running programme I took the Warwickshire players round the boundary at Bradford, where rain had prevented play for that day. As we loped round, several of the Yorkshire players were standing in the bar, with pint pots in their hands, telling us how daft we were. Just a few years later, everyone in the first-class game now takes part in running – the simplest, most effective way of warding off fatigue.

I hope that Bradford anecdote is some consolation to any club cricketers whose legs are pulled by their team-mates because they do their daily running. The dressing-room wag will say, 'Who do you think you are – Bob Willis'; yet he might be grateful to you for getting a breakthrough when no one else wants to bowl and the opposition need a handful of runs to win. If you discipline yourself to a daily run, you will be a more resilient, reliable and effective fast bowler – and who will be laughing at you then?

SPRINT TRAINING

This helps the fast bowler summon up that explosiveness which delivers the ball like the crack of a rifle shot. It tests out the leg and thigh muscles and the powers of recovery.

Start off with 'box' training. Make a square, each side measuring 30 yards. Walk the first side briskly, sprint the second, jog the third and make the final one at three-quarter pace, stretching out the legs with long arm movements as if you are pulling on a rope. Do this ten times.

Then do some sprints. Measure out the length of your run-up – say 30 yards. Sprint that distance, walk back and do it again. Do that 20 times. Sprint training is hard work if you are on your own, with no one to push you, so rest for a moment if the head spins and the legs start to wobble. Then do some longer sprints – between 75 and 100 yards. Take about 15 yards to slow down after passing the finish marker, then walk back purposefully and sprint again. Aim for ten of these. Make sure that you are fully warmed up before doing any sprint work – hamstrings and groins can easily tear unless they have been stretched.

Again there is nothing to stop any fast bowler of any age from trying sprint sessions. They stand you in good stead late in the day when you have to turn and chase a ball that has passed you. Although you have put in a long bowling stint, you owe it to the other bowlers to be as conscientious in the field as you expect them to be when it is your turn to bowl. Do a different sprinting session every day – 'box' training one day, the 30-yards sprint the following day and then the longer one.

STRETCHING EXERCISES

These are the ones loved by picture editors in Fleet Street and television directors. They seem to think it unusual to observe hulking great guys swinging their arms around them and contorting themselves into strange postures. The stretching exercises may look bizarre to the uninitiated but they are very important in attaining the necessary suppleness before trying to bowl fast. There are 15 of them and they take up just ten minutes of your time.

(1) Begin with your legs wide apart, swinging both arms to the left, then the right. Look at the hands as they go past your face. The feet must be flat on the ground and avoid doing this too quickly. A good one for loosening the upper torso. 20 times.

Bernard Thomas is a useful man to have around just before net practice. Ten good stretches with either leg soon reveals if the groin is weak!

(2) Now swing your arms from the sides to the front and join them together; back again to the sides. 20 times.

(3) With your arms stretched out in front, take them to the sides, then round over your head to the front again. Make sure the upper parts of the arms touch your ears as the arms go backwards. 20 times.

(4) Hands at the back of the neck and legs apart. Stretch to the left 20 times and the same for the right. Do this slowly for maximum advantage. Feel the muscles in the side loosen up – a side injury can put you out of action for upwards of a month, so do this one very conscientiously.

(5) Stretch the arms high over the head and bend to either side ten times. A good one for the back, shoulder and side muscles.

(6) Feet apart, stretch out the arms in front of you. Press back four times then take the arms down to the outside of the left foot and press down another four times. Do the same between your legs. Repeat for the right side of your body. Ten times each side.

(7) Take the weight on your left foot and stretch out your back leg behind you. Stretch the groin ten times, slowly and deliberately. Turn round and repeat the exercise with the right foot taking the weight. The groin is a very vulnerable area for a fast bowler and this exercise is invaluable.

(8) Place the feet together, with the arms on either side. Push the arms forward to a 90-degree angle, then bring them back and up above your head. Get up on tip-toe for the stretching and feel your shoulders going back. 20 times.

(9) Again place the feet together. Put the left foot over the right one and press down ten times to the floor. Keep the back arched and stretch slowly with the fingers pointing downwards. Change feet and also do it ten times. An excellent one for hamstrings.

(10) Stand up straight. Grasp your right foot and let the left leg take the strain with the left hip pushed forward. Pull the right leg back ten times, feeling the thigh muscle stretching. Repeat for the left leg.

(11) Take a wide stride. Press the arms down in front and count to four. Swing the arms left to the outside of the foot, then to the right. Come up and press the arms back past the head. Arch the back and really push those arms back. Ten times in all.

(12) With your legs wide apart, place your hands on your hips and roll the body from side to side 15 times.

(13) Place the hands at the back of your head and describe a circle round your body with your head. Ten times.

(14) Roll your right shoulder and arm round ten times. Repeat for the left shoulder.

(15) Turn the neck from left to right slowly, then try to lift up your head as far as you can. Then turn your neck from right to left and repeat. Ten times either side.

The most important of these 15 simple exercises are those that loosen the arms and shoulders and those involving the hamstring and groin. They are extremely worthwhile just before play begins, especially if it is cold and you want to bowl fast without tweaking a hamstring or tearing a shoulder muscle. A club side could easily do them together half an hour before the game starts: if one chap does them on his own he will probably be ridiculed by his mates, so why not help each other out?

All the exercises I have outlined are vital to the first-class cricketer and I would like to think they are helpful to the club fast bowler who wants to improve his standard of performance. The growth of one-day cricket has really brought home to the professionals that suppleness, strength and staying-power are essential.

Before the advent of limited-overs cricket, the professional fast bowler would bowl himself to peak fitness out in the middle, playing more than 30 matches that lasted three days each. He deserved his day off on Sunday. In the last 20 years, athleticism in the field has become the criterion of the successful one-day side and, although the fast bowler does not have to bowl so many overs, he is still under physical strain in a limited-overs match. Bowling eight overs off a reduced run-up can be very tiring, especially at the end of an innings: the fast bowler will then be dealing in only 'effort' balls at that stage, where he pitches it up to the batsman or drops it short of a length, in both cases to restrict the scoring opportunities. Either way, he has to find that little bit extra for the yorker or the short-pitched delivery, with the consequent danger of over-stepping the mark and getting no-balled.

I would like to think the attitude to fitness by modern first-class cricketers is one department that is getting through to club players. The dramatic upsurge in the amount of jogging in this country in recent years makes me believe that more and more people no longer care about being leg-pulled because they take exercise. Equally it does not appear strange anymore to see a cricketer train without having a bat or ball in his hand. Many a midsummer match is now won by someone gutsy enough to run through dimly-lit streets on winter mornings.

Club players who have trained hard in the winter should take it easy at the start of the season, especially if it is cold and damp: the risk of a pulled muscle or stiffness is then very real. Try not to slip yourself too soon. It is just like driving a car with a cold engine: you cannot race away until it warms up. Get to know your own body, because everyone has a different bowling action which brings its own physical pressure in some part of the body. Find out where you are vulnerable and try to strengthen the part. The wear and tear of fast bowling does take its eventual toll, but you can – with intelligence and foresight – keep yourself as fit as possible.

Organise your training programme: work out your schedule and follow it to the letter. It will help if you can train alongside a team-mate or friend as healthy competition and encouragement can get you over the hurdles of pain. Tell yourself that each new stage of fitness is another step towards improving as a fast bowler. Try for variety in your training to help stave off boredom – a game of squash or a swim, for example. It helps if you play other sports in the winter; non-contact ones like badminton, squash and hockey keep you toned up and in a better condition for working towards fast-bowling fitness.

Another thing to think about is your diet. You need a controlled amount of foods and fluids to build up energy and to replace the fluids, sugars and salts you lose during a hard, long spell of bowling. For the club cricketer who plays in the

An example of the wear and tear suffered by all fast bowlers if they play for long enough. On the left, my left knee is fairly straight and able to take the weight of my delivery. Compare the situation after two cartilage operations – I have had to adjust the position of the left leg to avoid buckling.

afternoon, I would recommend a lunch of carbohydrate-based foods that will convert quickly to energy and stave off that heavy-legged feeling we all experience at some stage. For an adult a pint of beer before a match is not a bad idea, as long as it does not make you too sleepy – the high carbohydrate content yields energy. On the other hand, the goodness from a big juicy steak takes too long to convert into energy. On the day of a game, take some extra sugar in your tea or breakfast cereal or have some ice cream – that keeps the sugar content from running too low in the muscles and wards off lethargy. A couple of glucose tablets will also help fuel intensive effort by increasing blood sugar. Finally, drink plenty of water to avoid dehydration.

All that sprinting, twisting, straining and stretching really tests out a fast bowler's pain threshold and morale. You must expect to be niggled by minor aches, otherwise you are not putting enough effort into your bowling. Eventually you become immune to the aches and pains but it is a different matter with a serious injury. Deep down you will know if you are seriously injured and then you should take advice and get immediate treatment. Watch out in particular for stress or fatigue injuries which occur in bones and ligaments and result from overwork. They become very painful because the sufferer tends to carry on using the damaged area – it could be shin soreness, trouble in the base of the spine or in the achilles tendon. The sooner they are treated the better as you cannot continue bowling through such injuries for very long. The knee is another dangerous area, as I know to my cost: I have had two major knee operations and on each occasion my career was only saved by brilliant surgery. Routine knee-cartilage operations are fairly common and the important thing here is to get the cartilage removed before the knee is badly damaged. It is then a case of building up the wasted muscles as soon as you can.

Already I have conditioned myself to an old age where I cannot move as freely as contemporaries who were nowhere near as fit as me when we were in our prime. The repeated minor injuries I have accumulated in bowling fast will just add up: arthritis in the hip, shoulder and ankles looks likely and I imagine my knees will not be terribly sound. I shall try to minimize the pain by keeping as active as I can and ploughing on with my running, but the tissues and joints will protest at all the effort I have demanded from them. I view that eventuality philosophically, because I would never have stayed at the top in international cricket unless I had sorted out my attitude to training. My mind used to wander on the field, purely because fatigue sapped my concentration. Achieving fitness changed all that and made me a much better fast bowler. The same principle applies to anyone else.

6
BOWLING ON DIFFERENT WICKETS

A fast bowler has to adapt to the various types of wickets he will encounter during a season. On occasions, he will be able to bowl at his fastest and get full reward from the pitch for the effort put in, yet far too often for my liking he will be frustrated by a slow wicket with little bounce. In such circumstances, strength of character becomes almost as vital as technique and the fast bowler needs to exercise his brain to assess the best way to triumph over the conditions.

At any level of the game, much mumbo-jumbo is talked about wickets. Even in first-class cricket, you can see the so-called experts on their haunches staring at the wicket, prodding it and making rash statements. I know very few first-class cricketers who can consistently read a wicket correctly; most of us get our prognostications wrong at some stage in the season. In club cricket, the urge to offer glib forecasts seems even more prevalent: players who have picked up the appropriate jargon from the media rattle on about the ball 'going through the top' without much idea of what it all means. I suppose this apparent knowledge is a manifestation of the club cricketer's keenness for the game – most of us are loath to admit we have hardly a clue about how a wicket will play. That is no consolation to the captain, who has to make a decision if he wins the toss, and to the fast bowler who has to work out his line of attack pretty quickly if he is to start the match. There is the additional worry about the weather – in club cricket, most wickets are left exposed to the elements and a mid-afternoon shower can change the character of the pitch drastically.

The ideal wicket for any class of cricket is one with an even spread of closely shaved grass on it and a hard surface. It should yield an even bounce throughout, favouring the fast bowler in the early stages and helping the spinners more and more as the match progresses. The pitch should be fast throughout, giving encouragement to both the fast bowler and the spinner who needs bounce to ensure any snicks carry to his close fielders. I really do not understand why groundsmen cannot produce more of such wickets. I appreciate that the weather in England causes havoc with a groundsman's preparation but this is a scientific age and surely there are sufficient gadgets to help him? In first-class cricket, the players tend to get obsessional about poor wickets. We get the blame for poor, unimaginative cricket – and rightly so – but I do believe that groundsmen get off lightly when such criticism is being handed out publicly. I could guarantee a better, more exciting standard of performance from first-class cricketers if the pitches were truer and faster.

Such surfaces in club cricket are like oases in a desert, and for many good reasons. There is simply not enough time, money and expertise available. Most clubs do not possess adequate covering and so the pitches are at the mercy of the weather, thereby ruining the chance of an even texture of grass. Justifiably, club players want to get out there and play at weekends, so rare words of caution about ruining the surface are spurned. The same applies if it rains during the game: most want to carry on unless it becomes a downpour. Any profits from the clubhouse bar are usually given over to new equipment or sightscreens, rather than to covers or acquiring expert advice on pitches. All this is very understandable and reflects the proper desire to play the game for fun, but the club player cannot therefore complain if the standard of wicket is poor.

I believe club wickets should always favour batsmen because that is the way bowlers learn to improve their skills. It is also safer – watching moderate players suffering on dangerous wickets is not at all funny. Unfortunately the bulk of club wickets tend to be slow ones with little bounce, enabling the limited stroke-maker to push forward and accumulate runs while the fast bowler gets more and more frustrated. This is when the fast bowler has to use his brains and pitch the ball up: speed through the air will always be a real handful, irrespective of the wicket's flatness, but bouncers become a waste of time because they will just sit up to be smashed. The batsman has much more time to judge the pace of a bouncer on a slow wicket and they are not really worth the effort involved. In these circumstances, use the new ball as well as you can, look after the shine and rely on changes of pace and swinging it through the air at speed. Block the scoring strokes through the covers and be patient, waiting for the batsman's mistake.

It is just as important to be cool and rational when the wicket helps the fast bowler. Sometimes there may have been too much grass left on the wicket so that the ball deviates at speed once the seam has gripped the grassy surface; other times the pitch may be two-paced, with one delivery scuttling through very low and the next taking off from a length. That kind of wicket is the most dangerous one on which to play cricket: it normally happens after rain, when a hot sun is drying a surface that has been exposed to the downpour. In this case, the fast bowler must remember that the batsman will probably not be adequately protected, that his reactions are not those of a highly trained athlete and that everyone on the pitch is supposedly playing for sheer enjoyment. Drop your pace, pitch the ball well up to the bat and use your common sense: nobody wants a serious injury and wickets are just as likely to fall if you rely on yorkers and late swing, rather than digging it in short and watching the batsman hop frantic-ally around. How would you like the same treatment when it is your turn to bat?

The same necessity for sensible bowling applies when the wicket is less dangerous, but the ball is seaming about all over the place – it is then far too easy to get excited and spray the ball around, rather than waiting for the conditions to help you. The mind tends to wander because subconsciously you relax; after all, the wicket is in your favour, so you are bound to pick up a cheap haul. The runs start trickling away, the batsmen play and miss frequently, yet hang on. One or two misfields off your bowling do nothing to improve your mood as it dawns on you that the side's reliance on your ability might have been misplaced: perhaps the slow medium-pacer is going to replace you unless you capitalize on the conditions pretty quickly. There is no use steaming in and bowling at your fastest. Concentrate on hitting the seam and let the grassy wicket do the rest: remember the basics of technique and avoid rushing up to the bowling crease. Do not pitch it too short – line and length are more important on this day, rather than pinging the ball around the batsman's ears.

On a wicket favouring the batsman – lacking pace and bounce – the good fast bowler should still be a handful because he is concentrating hard. The margin of error is that much narrower and any slight variation in line and length will be punished, so you must work out your tactics very quickly. You must provide your own encouragement and exert your will over the proceedings. The same applies when you encounter a fast, bouncy wicket: avoid the temptation to try to knock the batsman's head off all the time. If the bounce is even, the wicket will favour the bat just as much as the ball. A little push off the front foot will guide the ball through the covers and a crack of the wrists will mean a delicate cut to the boundary. The class batsman uses the pace of a fast bowler's delivery to steer the ball away from the fielders and a good wicket will do wonders for his confidence, even if you manage to whistle a few round his ears. Remember that a ball pitching halfway on a fast, bouncy pitch is harmless: the batsman can either score off it, or step back and watch it sail harmlessly over his head. To get the kind of bounce which tucks up the batsman and makes him fend off the ball to the close fielders, you need to pitch it up three-quarters of the way down the pitch. Remember that the surprise factor is essential for a successful bouncer.

Think about your field placings to get the best out of a particular wicket. On a reasonable pitch with some early bounce, the fast bowler's job is to get batsmen out quickly, before the ball loses its shine and the pitch starts to get placid. An attacking field is a priority, so leave third man, mid-off and mid-on vacant: there is time enough to block the scoring shots and save runs later, but this is the time to take wickets. If you are quick enough, use four slips and a gully; a man in the

1 FAST BOWLER ON TRUE WICKET

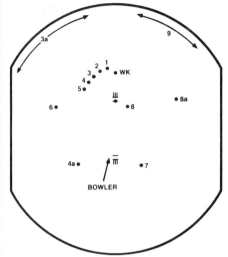

1 First slip 2 Second slip 3 Third slip 4 Fourth
slip 5 Gully 6 Cover 7 Mid-on 8 Forward short
leg 9 Long leg
3a Third man 4a Mid-off 8a Square leg

2 FAST BOWLER ON SLOW WICKET

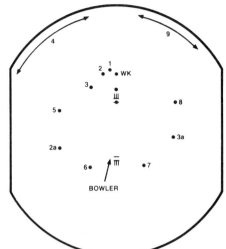

1 First slip 2 Second slip 3 Gully 4 Third man
5 Cover 6 Mid-off 7 Mid-on 8 Square leg
9 Long leg
2a Extra cover 3a Mid-wicket

3 FAST-MEDIUM BOWLER OF OUTSWING

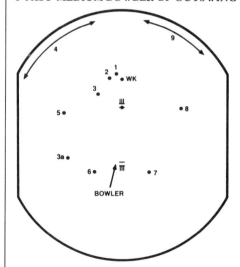

1 First slip 2 Second slip 3 Gully 4 Third man
5 Cover 6 Mid-off 7 Mid-on 8 Square leg
9 Long leg
3a Extra cover

4 FAST-MEDIUM BOWLER OF INSWING

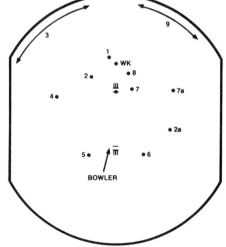

1 First slip 2 Gully 3 Third man 4 Cover
5 Mid-off 6 Mid-on 7 Short leg 8 Leg slip
9 Long leg
2a Mid-wicket 7a Square leg

Diagrams 1 to 5 offer general guidelines for the bowler who should always be ready to experiment to find the field-settings which suit him best. In each diagram, numbers 1 to 9 apply to the typical field-settings in first-class cricket. Club and school cricketers may well have to dispense with some of their close-in fielders, alternative positions being denoted by 3a, 4a etc.

5 SEAM BOWLER ON HELPFUL WICKET

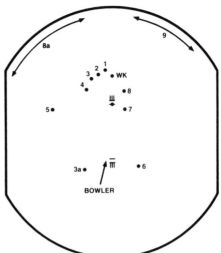

1 First slip 2 Second slip 3 Third slip 4 Gully
5 Cover 6 Mid-on 7 Forward short leg
8 Backward short leg 9 Long leg
3a Mid-off 8a Third man

6 DEFENSIVE FIELD

Diagram 6 shows a typical defensive field as adopted in limited-overs cricket, when at least four fielders (excluding the bowler and wicketkeeper) must remain within the circle. If mid-off or mid-on – or both – have to drop back, then third man or long leg – or both – will move inside the circle.

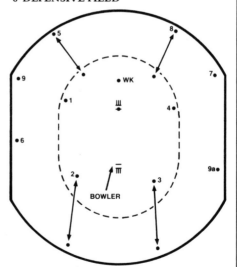

1 Deep gully 2 Mid-off 3 Mid-on 4 Square leg
5 Third man 6 Deep extra cover 7 Deep
backward square leg 8 Long leg 9 Deep square
third man (if attacking the off stump)
9a Deep mid-wicket (if attacking the leg stump)

bat/pad position close in on the leg side for the short-pitched delivery; a leg-slip for the one that comes in off the seam; a long leg for the mistimed hook and the safe push off the legs; and a man in the covers to stop the singles and give chase for the drive. The fast bowler must bowl to this field – accuracy and speed have to work in harmony. The outswinger should be his stock ball, with an occasional inswinger and bouncer for variety. The slower ball could be risky in such circumstances – he might be played away through the wide open spaces with some comfort if the slower ball is misdirected.

Once the wicket starts to lose its early fire, it is time to be sensible without going on the defensive. The leg-slip would go out to square leg and the man at bat/pad to mid-on. Perhaps two of the slips would go to third man and mid-off. Keep the mid-off position open as long as possible: with the new ball, your basic aim is to bowl outswingers from a full length and you want to tempt the batsman to play a shot by leaving an exposed area at mid-off. If you bowl half-volleys, you will be punished by a good off-driver, but that is a calculated risk. You must attack and tempt the batsman.

On a helpful wicket – where the ball is seaming around quickly – make sure you keep the bat/pad and leg-slip all the time. If you are making the ball hit the seam consistently, then the chances are that it will move in on the batsman just as much as away from the bat, so you must not have an unbalanced field. There is no merit in bowling wicked 'in-dippers' if most of your close fielders are on the off side. On a wet wicket – where the ball stands up off a length almost vertically – post another man at forward short-leg for the delivery that a batsman cannot keep down. Make sure the gully and fourth slip are a little more forward than usual, because a ball that comes off the glove does not carry so far as off the bat. The same applies on a slow wicket: because the ball does not hit the bat all that quickly, it follows that a defensive stroke will not travel very far. Your slips and gully should come a couple of paces forward.

What should you look for when examining the wicket before a match? For a start, you could assume that most of your team-mates do not really know what they are talking about as they walk up and down, saying things like 'Hey! Look at this crack – I don't fancy batting on this!' or 'I reckon it'll turn square today, skipper!' Snap judgements like 'It's a good track – 450 runs in the match today' often look a shade wide of the mark when the pints are being pulled a few hours later in the clubhouse as the top-scorer modestly talks you through his 30 runs. The only man I knew who approached infallibility at assessing a wicket was dear old Kenny Barrington, who managed England on several tours before he tragically died of a heart attack. Both at home and abroad, Kenny would use his faithful penknife on the wicket. He would stick it in the turf as far as possible, draw it out and examine how much moisture was on the knife. If it was dampish, you could bet that the ball would seam around a lot in the early stages, possibly for the whole of the match; if the knife was dry, the pitch would become easier and slower as the game progressed. Kenny invariably got it right.

There are obvious things to look out for, however, without having recourse to the Barrington method. If the pitch is damp with plenty of grass on it, then it should be ideal for the seam bowler because the turf will grip the seam. If it is brown and hard, it has a chance of being a good cricket wicket, with something in it for the stroke player, the fast bowler and the spinner: the medium-pacers will have to wait for another day. If the wicket is very dry and dusty with a few cracks on a length, the fast bowler can look forward to a rest: all he will be expected to do is get the shine off the ball for the slow bowlers to grip it properly.

The big responsibility comes when the team captain decides to put the opposition in after examining the pitch and working out his options. In effect he is saying that his opening bowlers are good enough to win the match for him, to take advantage of the grassy conditions. Such a move has become more and more prevalent in modern Test cricket, an apt comment on the poor wickets that have been prepared. Club cricketers – following the customs of their international heroes – tend to follow suit and aim for a decisive early breakthrough. The fast bowler must be able to deal with such pressures, working out his field beforehand and operating closely with his captain. If the ploy backfires, that is usually the fault of the opening bowlers. Concentration and calmness are therefore critical qualities in the first hour of the game. As each over passes, the batsmen will feel more secure and the psychological impetus will pass from the fielding side. The batting side's quick bowlers will be watching keenly how the wicket is behaving and planning their line of attack. The fielders will start to fret and the main strike weapon will worry about letting them down. How the fast bowler copes with that kind of responsibility will shape the result of the match.

I believe the modern fad of inserting the opposition in first-class cricket would never have happened if the wickets had been better prepared. The traditional view has always been that both sides should take a chance with the elements by leaving the wickets uncovered. This is all very well if the wicket is good enough at the start of the game with a uniform bounce and an encouraging amount of pace so that the contest between bat and ball is decided by superior skill and technique. That is just not so anymore: too many wickets in English first-class cricket are green and underprepared, offering a disproportionate amount of encouragement to the 'phantom seamer', the chap who wobbles the ball about at just over medium pace and relies on the conditions to do a lot of the work for him. The game was meant to be dominated by contrasting skills – majestic attacking batsmen, the subtlety of slow bowling and the raw aggression of the quick bowler. Counties are getting one-eyed about winning trophies and they instruct their groundsmen to prepare wickets that suit their complement of bowlers, rather than reflect the variety which should be in cricket. The problem is now a world-wide one. Having toured with England since 1970, I can vouch for the fact that wickets are getting slower and slower all over the world. Some are dreadfully prepared and dangerous, but the bulk of them are lifeless and dispiriting. I cannot understand why groundsmen allow this to happen. What is wrong with digging up the square every few years? I believe that wickets simply die of old age and that they should regularly be dug up and a fresh start made.

Something must be done about wickets, because the game is getting too uniform for my taste. It affects the club scene also – the habits of the professional game seep down to the grass roots, I am sure. Club cricketers go to county and Test matches and see what is being played on the appropriate pitches and they are led to believe that this is the way the game should be structured. The out-standing club players of today are the county cricketers of tomorrow and unless they are learning their trade on good, fast wickets they will never be outstanding. Covered wickets would at least allow them the chance to develop those skills, provided the wicket itself is true.

I suppose a fast bowler gets more irate about slow wickets than his team-mates because he is keyed up to bowl quickly and ends up being frustrated by a feather-bed which prevents the ball getting stump-high. I still get very depressed about lifeless pitches, but not nearly as much as in my early days in first-class cricket. I would mentally throw in the towel on certain days, partly through frustration at the pitch and partly because I realised I was not fit enough to battle on. It took a great West Indian fast bowler to force me into thinking positively about slow wickets. The pitch for the Oval Test of 1976 was as dead as they come and West Indies made 687 on a surface that drove me to distraction. As the match progressed the bounce got lower and lower and the teeth of the fast bowlers were drawn. All except one, Michael Holding. With a beautifully lithe run-up, he generated real pace to take 14 wickets. Nine of them were clean bowled – a tribute to his speed through the air. In contrast, I took one wicket in the match and conceded an average of six runs an over, blaming it all on the dreadfully slow pitch. Holding's performance made me realize that there is absolutely no point in allowing the state of the wicket to distract a fast bowler; instead, he must make the best of what he has got. Good fast bowlers perform better when their pride is at stake and the conditions are not favourable; they regulate their thinking to the challenge set by the wicket. Never give in to the temptation to moan about the conditions. A positive attitude can surmount many disadvantages in cricket.

7

THE FAST BOWLER AND HIS CAPTAIN

The fast bowler is the team's potential matchwinner, but he should not be over-worked for that reason. He must be captained firmly, sympathetically and with specialist care: sometimes he will need a rocket, on other occasions a sympathetic word. He should never be overbowled, so that he cannot come back and bowl fast later in the day; the captain who understands that will have the respect of his fast bowler. If he believes his captain has his best interests at heart, the fast bowler will subconsciously find that little bit of extra inspiration when the going is rough.

The greatest skill in captaining fast bowlers is knowing when to tell them to take a rest. Every fast bowler with enough pride and commitment always wants another over, knowing he is getting tired but remaining convinced that just one more over will land the fish he has been angling for in the last half-hour. The temptation for the captain is to give in and let his quickie get his own way. That certainly seems to be the case in club cricket, where the fast bowler is often criminally overbowled, sending down up to 20 overs in a row without respite. That is ridiculous for all concerned – the sharp cutting edge of the attack is blunted and the rest of the side loses confidence in a captain who lacks the strength of character to put the fast bowler in his place. The donkey work should be done by the medium-pacer or the spinner, not the fastest bowler in the team.

The captain needs to be a bit of a psychologist with his fast bowler, to under-stand his character. If he has conceded 20 runs in the first two overs and the wicket is playing slowly, the fast bowler needs help and reassurance. Even if he has bowled badly at that stage he needs encouragement, to feel that his captain is behind him and not wondering how soon he can take him off in favour of the medium-pacer who will block up an end. Unless he feels confident, the quickie's performance will deteriorate, so the occasional white lie from the captain sometimes does not go amiss. He should move to mid-on or mid-off to be near his struggling bowler, ready to offer soothing words or tactical guidance as he walks back to his mark, wondering where the ball will possibly pitch next. Everyone in the fielding side should realize that they are in trouble if their quick bowler has to be taken off when the ball is still new: a collective effort to boost his confidence is necessary and the captain should ensure that this is forthcoming. I am not suggesting that he should be cossetted all the time like a prima-donna, simply that everything ought to be done to help him bowl fast and accurately when he is needed.

Like the other players, the fast bowler should know the tactical requirements of the match. The strategy should have been explained in the dressing-room, so that the bowlers know what is expected of them. If the wicket is likely to play slowly, the fast bowler will be asked for an early blast with the new ball; on a pitch set to take spin, the fast bowler will be particularly useful against batsmen who relish the challenge of slow bowling. He should be wheeled up whenever such a player comes to the crease, while the slow bowler is left to concentrate on those who cannot tackle his wiles so confidently. This ploy is used in Test cricket more times than people realise and if the fast bowler manages to dismiss the good player of spin bowling, he has played a vital role. Some wickets are more important to get than others and the fast bowler should know that the object of the exercise is for his team to get ten wickets and win, rather than seven for himself and a draw. When he has managed an important breakthrough that fits in with the captain's strategy, he should be thanked and given his sweater: nobody should expect to be given a couple more overs simply because he has just taken a wicket.

Field placing is always a potential area of conflict between fast bowler and captain. One may think more defensively than the other – whilst the bowler may be worried about his analysis, the skipper might be more concerned about attacking the batsman and placing extra close fielders for the snicks, rather than a third man or deep square-leg. Neither should ever think about setting a field for bad bowling; if there is a likelihood of two bad balls an over the fast bowler should not really be used. The conventional attacking field is six men on the off side and three on the leg side – or even seven and two – and the fast bowler should stick to the usual field until the batsman's particular style of playing has been assessed. The captain should put the onus on his bowler if he insists on a specific field, telling him that he can have what he wants as long as he bowls to the desired line. That should instill a sense of responsibility in the bowler and keep him thinking, rather than fizzing the ball all over the place.

Both captain and fast bowler must keep an eye out for the batsman's idio-syncrasies. If he is looking to get off the mark by tickling the ball down to fine leg, post a fine leg-slip for the catch. If he is playing with too much right hand, bring another man into the gully region for a possible catch. Never hesitate to alter the field if you have a good reason for doing so. The best piece of captaincy advice I ever received came from Geoff Boycott, who told me, 'If you think of something, do it right away, don't wait for an over.' He is right – there is nothing more frustrating than to see a batsman play a ball in the air in an area you had thought about filling with a fielder. At the same time, do not be tempted to 'follow the ball'. Just because a batsman has played a ball through the covers for four does not mean he will do the same again off the next delivery – indeed the odds against that happening are very high. The fast bowler might say that he wants to take out one of his slips to cover that gap but he must be resisted, especially if the ball is still swinging and he is attacking. The captain should point out that boundaries through the covers are inevitable and that he should continue bowling to his field. Following the ball by immediate field alterations is a sign of bad and unimaginative captaincy and it shows a lack of confidence in the bowler's ability. The point should be made firmly but calmly, for there is nothing more embarrassing than open disagreement between bowler and captain, with the rest of the side watching the hands being waved, the voices raised and the fast bowler stalking back angrily to his mark.

The captain should always watch out for any change in mood from his quickie, who is bound to get wound up sometimes. The fast bowler who reacts calmly to every circumstance on the field will normally lack fire in his belly and, provided the histrionics are kept to the minimum, he should let off steam as he walks back to his mark. His captain should observe how quickly he manages to recover his self-control before delivering the ball, if necessary telling him to walk back a little slower, to take a few deep breaths and think out his tactics. Tantrums and intimidation can easily be nipped in the bud with a few choice words. I know of no fast bowler who remains emotionally controlled throughout a stint and when he gets excited and keyed-up it is a sign that he is trying hard. The captain has to take that state of mind into consideration if he has words with his fast bowler on the field of play. Things can be said in the heat of the moment over something like field-placings or the bowler's lack of accuracy and just because the fast bowler blasts back with a defensive sentence or two does not mean he disrespects his skipper – simply that he is getting stuck into his bowling and is a little on edge.

Tactical advice from the captain ought to be given to the fast bowler when necessary. That guidance might not be taken seriously by the bowler, but at least he will be psychologically boosted by the knowledge that his skipper is trying to get the best out of him. Occasionally, he should stand in the slips to watch his fast bowler in order to see how he is bowling, whether he is hitting the seam or putting in the necessary effort. He may spot that the bowling hand is not directly behind the ball at the moment of delivery, that his arm is not as high as it should be or that he loses rhythm in his run-up. The fast bowler may be so wrapped up in his bowling that he fails to observe certain idiosyncrasies in the batsman's methods. The captain should be ready with advice at all times. If, for instance, he notices that the batsman's instinctive movement is on to the front foot, he might suggest that his bowler pitches the ball just a little bit shorter. The skipper should also encourage the wicket-keeper to offer suggestions to the fast bowler. The keeper is in the best position of all to judge how he is bowling and vocal encouragement from him after a good delivery is much appreciated by any fast bowler. The rest of the fielders ought to look after the ball and shine it, so that it will continue to swing; if anyone stops the ball with his boot when a hand could have done the same, the captain should give him a rocket. At the fall of a wicket, the ball should be tossed to the player who is acknowledged to be the best shiner of the ball in the side – as someone who is not a great shiner, I appreciate the amount of work that can be done on the ball during those couple of minutes' wait for the new batsman.

Every fast bowler has a different pain threshold and a captain should know how far he can be pushed. Assuming that the bowler wants to keep going, the difficulty is knowing how effective he is going to be with that bruised heel, sore toe, strained shoulder or bad back. If the bowler is reluctant to bowl because of an injury, the captain should be ready to examine the real motives behind that reluctance. Is it a minor injury, or is it that the bowler merely does not relish the prospect of a long, hard bowl on a flat, slow wicket in hot weather? Whatever the circumstances, the captain must be alive to the situation and be prepared to cajole the reluctant bowler or bully him through an over to take his mind off the pain. The fielders should also have been alerted to the situation and must actively encourage the injured fast bowler. A fast bowler must learn to accept niggling pains as part of the job and put them to the back of his mind. It is part of the captain's responsibility to try to get him into the right frame of mind if he lacks that mental resolve.

Can a fast bowler also be a successful captain? History supports the view that it is difficult to combine both jobs at the highest level in the game. Certainly the logistics are against the fast bowler/captain: most of us are pretty whacked at the end of our over and it is very difficult to switch one's mind back to the tactical nuances of the game. You may have been concentrating very hard at keeping a batsman on his back foot throughout most of the over, then hustling through a fast yorker to catch him in the wrong position. When the batsman has survived the last ball of the over your initial thoughts, as you pull on your sweater, breathing heavily after the effort involved, are still on your contest-within-the-contest as you plod off to your place in the field. It is very easy to forget that you also have the next over to think about: organizing the field for the left-hander, remembering to give a word of encouragement to the bowler at the other end, wondering how much longer you should carry on at your end. In limited-overs cricket it becomes even more difficult as you try to keep track of the runs-per-over equation. At some stage in a match all hell breaks loose on the field and the captain must be fully alert and ready to make instant decisions and guide the team calmly through the crisis. The job is that more exacting if he is also the team's strike bowler who has to galvanize himself into a peak of effort and concentration. He then has three jobs in the field, those of fast bowler, fielder and captain, compared to the batsman who only need concern himself with fielding and captaincy. It is thus much easier for the batsman to be the cool, controlled type on the field than a fast bowler.

I would not recommend captaincy for a young fast bowler, who has enough on his plate learning how to tackle a demanding task as he gets older, without having to think through the complexities of the overall tactics of the match. Ideally a fast bowler should combine his physical commitment with the kind of thought and tactical awareness you would expect from a captain, but that is asking a lot of someone who also has to be the fittest in the team, the chap who has to relish the responsibility of leading the attack. However, once a fast bowler has come to terms with all these demands, I see no reason why he should not extend his responsibilities to those of captaincy: the ability to lead from the front and win matches by personal example will always gain the team's respect. I was lucky that the captaincy of England and Warwickshire did not come my way until I was over 30. By that time I had worked out my bowling and knew to my own satisfaction my physical and technical limitations. I enjoyed getting completely involved in the team effort through being captain. Keeping my mind alert when physically tired was a demanding challenge, quite a contrast to the days when I would graze down at long leg during a bowling stint, wondering whether I would ever get my breath back and praying that the ball would stay away from my area. Anybody who has played first-class cricket for more than a decade should have accumulated enough experience to make a stab at captaincy, provided he has the backing and respect of his team. There is at least one advantage in choosing as skipper the team's strike bowler: he is worth his place in the side and his appointment does not upset the balance of the team, which sometimes happens when a batsman who is not in the top bracket is brought in.

As the day wears on, the strains on the fast-bowler/captain get more pronounced. In the first hour or so the tactical needs are fairly straightforward, in that the requirement is to get as many wickets as possible with the new ball and keep attacking. As the pitch gets flatter and the batsmen more assured, the challenge becomes greater: he has to dig deep into his physical reserves to bowl while keeping a tight tactical rein, whereas the batsman/captain would stand at slip thinking only about the development of his resources. The vice-captain and wicket-keeper become essential cogs in the wheel and must keep the fielders on their toes and not hesitate to point out something that has possibly been missed, even if the point has been already grasped. As England vice-captain to Mike Brearley, I was not the best number two when we were out on the field. I was too wrapped up in my bowling while we were out there, too worried about not turning in consistent enough performances to keep my place. I was always conscious that a vice-captain can be dropped far more painlessly than a captain in Test cricket. My loyalty and support were total, but on the field it was as a player rather than as number two to Brearley. When we were off the field I was much more like the conventional vice-captain, enjoying the responsibilities of organizing nets, instilling discipline into the squad and handing out a few rockets where they were deserved. I did my best to take the off-field pressure away from Mike, but the demands of fast bowling limited my contribution on the field. Yet when I became England captain I realized that the years spent as Brearley's vice-captain had been an instructive apprenticeship.

One of the major headaches a fast-bowler/captain faces is when to bowl himself again after his initial opening burst. There is a real possibility that he will bowl himself either too much or too little: he may feel that he should be the one to take the flak when a class batsman is settled, or he might think that his team-mates believe he is hogging the action. When someone else has done the hard work in mid-innings, a fast bowler exposes himself to accusations of selfishness if he brings himself back to mop up the tail and return an impressive analysis. In the first-class game team-mates will appreciate that the bowler most likely to get wickets at a particular stage of the innings should be used and more often than not it will be the main strike bowler. In club cricket, where some tail-enders are absolute suckers for any reasonable bowler, the fast-bowler/captain must be prepared to be flexible if the playing circumstances allow: perhaps a bowler has had an unlucky time of it lately and needs a few cheap wickets; it may be that a young, inexperienced bowler should be brought on to get a confidence-booster. He must never forget that others have given up their weekend to play for him and deserve something better than watching him selfishly terrorizing poor batsmen. If he is a good enough fast bowler, he will get enough wickets during the season when they are really needed by the team. School captains are even more vulnerable: the captain could easily be the only class fast bowler and he will need wisdom and character beyond his years to resolve the equation of winning the game, doing himself justice as a player and ensuring that others in the team benefit from matchplay. The kind of petty jealousies which befall most schoolboys and interference from a zealous cricket master can also complicate the situation.

On balance I would concede that it is more difficult for a fast bowler to captain a side successfully than a batsman. The job can, however, be done by a fast bowler if he enjoys his team's respect and unselfish support; if he has the character to make decisions that will not distract him from his bowling; and if he has the intelligence to view his bowling as part of a wider issue, not simply his sole justification for being out on the field. Admittedly these are fairly big ifs, but the task is perfectly possible.

8
FROM SCHOOLBOY TO COUNTY PROFESSIONAL

Any schoolboy fast bowler of ability has ambition: he dreams of playing the game for a living and, if he is very lucky, of representing his country. That was certainly my dream as I watched Brian Statham on television all those years ago instead of going upstairs to do my homework. At that time, however, I had no conception of the vast difference between doing well in school cricket and bowling at the best batsmen in the world. The gulf is enormous and you can only attempt to bridge it by making the very best of your available talent, hardening up your commitment towards fitness and assimilating the best of the advice you are offered.

By the time the fast bowler has started dominating school first elevens with his pace and hostility, his action has been worked out. (It usually stays the same throughout the rest of his career, give or take a few modifications. It takes a brave cricketer to strip down the model and drastically reconstitute it once he has proved the value of the original method in his current standard of cricket.) Fast bowling will be a fairly natural process for him and as he progresses in the game, attitude and temperament will become more vital: the attitude towards refining his technique and getting supremely fit, and the temperament needed to come to terms with the harsh realities of bowling at good batsmen on unhelpful wickets. The schoolboy who terrorizes 16-year-olds on dubious pitches has no chance of attaining the same sort of success in a superior standard of cricket unless he works at his game. As he progresses in the game, he needs to graft even harder to achieve the same results in the lower grade he has just left.

Cricket was the only thing I ever worked at at school. I was lucky to have a cricket master who was an MCC member and he instilled in me the necessary enthusiasm. I got into the school team two years ahead of my time and by the age of 15 I was playing club cricket. David Sydenham – the former Surrey opening bowler – was the captain of our school's old boys' team and he gave me invaluable advice and encouragement. I loved being the big fish in the small pool of school cricket while proceeding quietly through the club scene, taking it all in and learning how to bowl at adults. It was important to me to get into club cricket as soon as possible because I was bound to improve as long as I kept my eyes and ears open, but it was equally proper to remain loyal to my school, RGS Guildford, whenever I was selected. The good fortune I enjoyed makes me realize that so many naturally talented youngsters are lost to cricket because of chance circumstances – a mediocre cricket master, a lack of decent facilities, a dearth of good club cricket sides in the neighbourhood and even because the particular school does not have a cricket side.

Parents have to be careful that they do not push a boy too hard; he must not be set targets he cannot possibly achieve and they should simply let him enjoy his game, while getting stronger and growing to full height. The cricket master is so important because he has to maintain the keenness of his boys, rather than seem to have just a couple of favourites who are the best players at their age. Cricket is a terribly difficult game to organize during a 40-minute session in the school timetable because only a few manage to play a direct part, while the others simply stand around in the field. Many a youngster with talent has opted for other hobbies and sports because the cricket master could not keep him interested.

A sense of competition between schools is healthy as long as the ideal of winning does not get distorted. Healthy rivalry drags out the good performances from schoolboys mature enough to withstand the pressures and understand that sportsmanship and a sense of enjoyment are still worthwhile sporting philosophies. A properly controlled competitive streak prepares the talented schoolboy for the rigours of club cricket.

In club cricket, the drop-out rate among schoolboys is alarming. In some cases their own temperament is responsible – perhaps the extra competitiveness militates against a shy, retiring nature; at other times the older members of the club may be at fault. When a spotty adolescent joins a club he should be made to feel welcome, irrespective of his ability. Too many older players, jealous of a young challenger for the new ball, go out of their way to be unhelpful. Human nature can be cruel and some club cricketers resent a young rival who can bowl faster. His detractors will point out that the schoolboy sprays the ball about and that he tires easily: what they are really saying is that he should not take an established player's place. The boy may be ill at ease amid the worldly-wise camaraderie in the clubhouse bar, probably unable to understand many of the 'in-crowd' jokes and the apparent harshness of their judgements. If he is lucky, he will meet up with a few colleagues who are still in their teens and will play under a captain who is of the understanding type: he should be encouraged to improve and enjoy his cricket and not feel he has to be part of the wise-cracking clique. Eventually, his older team-mates will accept and like him, but initially the pressure is on the youngster to do himself justice in the nets and then on the field. That takes character and self-discipline. At some stage he will miss the inferior standard of school cricket, where he was a star and socially more at ease. How he tackles those pangs of nostalgia will determine his success at club level. If he really wants to improve, then he will work hard at the nets, ask the advice of the friendly seniors and tell himself he is a better cricketer for the sterner competition.

The young fast bowler will find that his analysis will suffer in his early days in club cricket. His speed will still get wickets but not so many batsmen will be as scared of him as the schoolboys of recent memory. Grizzled, craggy characters who are twice the youngster's age do not mind standing up and taking the ball on the body, so long as they see it through and smash the boy all over the ground as he tires. Brawny tail-enders will enjoy slogging him to parts of the field where the properly coached, correct schoolboys never stroked the ball. The young quickie has to learn how to take punishment, to bowl to his field and work out the best line to bowl at each particular batsman. Fully developed men can hit a cricket ball very hard indeed, irrespective of their natural batting ability, and that comes as a rude awakening to a schoolboy fast bowler used to seeing lads of his own age back away towards square leg when he sends down a particularly fast one. At this stage mature, understanding captaincy is essential: the boy should be rested when a renowned hitter comes to the crease and shows a relish for wayward fast bowling.

If the youngster is quick enough, lucky enough and sufficiently intelligent, he might force his way into first-class cricket, or at least play a couple of county second-eleven matches. A rude awakening is in store. If the gulf between school and club cricket is huge, well that between club and professional cricket is awesome. It is an achievement initially just to stop the batsman scoring: a maiden over is cause enough for a lap of honour to a young quickie. The batsmen are more sound defensively and no longer can you expect to get wickets with a fast, straight delivery. The wickets are better than the fliers on which you harvested so many wickets and the bat is invariably on top of the ball. You meet many good players on their way down in first-class cricket, men who have scored thousands of runs and countless centuries. Batsmen who have scored handsomely against international attacks in their heyday do not decline so drastically that they cannot thrash a raw, budding fast bowler. A ball that might easily have got you a wicket in the past will be arrogantly whipped away to the boundary. You become psychologically beaten when running in and unsure how to keep a class player quiet. Once you become worried, you find that you are not bowling to full potential and the battle seems to be lost. Some hard, realistic thinking is needed.

You should examine the line of your bowling for a start. In school and club cricket you aim for the stumps and rely on your speed, the unreliable wicket, or the batsman's slow reactions to get you wickets; any catches by slips or wicket-keeper are a bonus. It is totally different in county cricket: basically you aim for catches because most batsmen are not clean bowled, as their defences are so good. The county fast bowler looks to bowl in that 'halfway-house' area on a good wicket – getting the batsman half-back, half-forward and unsure of his bearings. I would say that 70 per cent of the fast bowler's deliveries in first-class cricket would not hit the stumps but bounce over the top. This difference in line has to be grasped as quickly as possible by every fast bowler who wants to earn a living in the game.

Once established in first-class cricket it is easy to forget how you used to bowl, as I learned to my cost once during a winter in South Africa. I had been a first-class cricketer for four years when I played club cricket in that winter, yet I was totally ineffectual: my 'halfway-house' deliveries were smashed away on good wickets by uncomplicated batsmen who liked to play shots. Unlike English county cricketers, they did not play defensively and were happy to carve my off-stump line over gully's head and through the covers off the back foot. If I had pitched the ball up more and aimed for the stumps I would have picked up many wickets through rash, attacking shots.

The other major problem when you are taken on to a county's staff is that of fatigue. You have to come to terms with bowling up to 30 overs a day against class players on flat wickets after a career of 15 overs on variable wickets against erratic batsmen. The physical strain is simply shattering, irrespective of your build. The young quickie may have a fine physique, but he still has to get himself fit for bowling in first-class cricket. It is a traumatic experience. Indeed, it took me almost a decade before I was satisfied with my level of fitness.

My early days at The Oval are etched in my memory and I recall them with anguish. I had come through the local system of talent-spotting: Surrey Schools, Surrey Colts and a game or two for the second eleven. I was pretty quick but the rough edges were there for all to see. Once on the Surrey staff, I would present myself at The Oval for a typical day of torture: bowling at the second eleven and then the first team for over an hour, grab a shower and watch the first-eleven game for the whole day. Arthur McIntyre, our coach, ensured that sitting watching the cricket was far from relaxing. He would creep up and quiz us about various aspects of the play and what we would have done in similar circumstances. If the answer was unimpressive, you were made to feel very small indeed and left wondering whether you had the mental aptitude for a career in first-class cricket, irrespective of your playing ability.

The time spent bowling in the nets was frightening. International players of the calibre of John Edrich, Ken Barrington, Mickey Stewart, Graham Roope and Younis Ahmed would really put me through the mangle. A defensive shot was a triumph and the slightest deviation in line or length was ruthlessly punished. I was forced to learn where to bowl at these batsmen to stop them shattering my confidence completely. In that respect, Arthur McIntyre's insistence that we watched every ball of the day's play was invaluable: he made us think about the game, to work out tactical ploys in our own minds. I managed to develop my memory for batsmen's weaknesses and Arthur's example has stayed with me throughout my career. I still try to watch all the play, whether in a Test or a county match, because you never stop learning. Regrettably, that is not a common attitude among younger players in first-class cricket. I have heard some of them say they do not like watching cricket because it is too boring! Such mental idleness shocks and saddens me. I fail to see how a cricketer of any standard can avoid improving his performance by watching closely how his superiors approach the complexities of the game. Dennis Lillee has always had my rapt attention because of his technical brilliance, yet one young fast-bowling colleague of mine on an Australian tour preferred to go off and play tennis rather than watch Lillee bowl. To me that is just incomprehensible and unprofessional.

A healthy attitude to learning is so important for a young fast bowler making his way in the game. He should never sit back and wait for people to tell him things. He ought to be asking questions of senior players, discarding nothing he has been told but picking out the bits that are particularly relevant to himself. Watch the best players in the nets and try to assess why they are the top bowlers or batsmen. Never forget that the speed at which you learn is more important than how much you are advised.

The coach is an integral part of your development once you get on the county staff. Like most individuals in charge of a group of sportsmen he is overworked, occasionally tetchy and has his own particular favourites but nonetheless he will be approachable, knowledgeable about the game and good at helping you to see things clearly and in perspective. You will be lucky if he has the ability to coach fast bowlers because that is an asset enjoyed by very few coaches in first-class cricket. The general opinion is that batting has far more facets and therefore needs greater attention from the coach. I disagree with that and the prevalence of coaches who used to be batsmen disturbs me. A fast bowler needs to be understood, to be chivied along at times and occasionally to be indulged: he is a proud, temperamental character with 'devil' in his soul who needs specific technical advice when things go wrong. Net practice in the county game seems to exist for the batsmen's benefit, rather than for the bowlers: we are there simply to play the batsmen into form and, if we are worried about our perform-ances, we have to go off and sort them out on our own or, if we are lucky, with the manager and a fellow fast bowler. I do concede that it is terribly difficult to coach fast bowlers. There are so many different ways used to bowl fast that there is no prototype for the coach to adopt as a standard. He might suggest extending the length of arm movement or speeding up the wrist action, but the majority of the best fast bowlers transgress at least some of the textbook essentials, making it almost impossible for the coach to point to someone who could be copied. The principles of batting are easier to coach because there are less imponderables involved.

Without the proper advice of a senior player at the right moment, I would have never played for England or made any real impact on the game. My saviour was John Edrich. I had just arrived on the Surrey staff and was getting stuck into some fruitless net bowling against the first-team stars when the coach Arthur McIntyre called a halt and gave me a lecture. He told me my action was far too open-chested and unorthodox and that it had to be changed. I had never been aware that my action was at all unusual, but obviously I took his remarks to heart and followed his advice. He told me how to bowl in the approved MCC-coaching-manual manner and I took it all in and set out to do just that. I ran up, remembered to place my right foot parallel to the bowling crease, turned my trunk round at the right moment and whipped into the delivery – and the ball went into the side of the net. I was humiliated and my confidence fell apart for weeks: my coach had told me in no uncertain terms that I was all wrong for fast bowling and I just could not master the textbook style. I expected to get the sack at the season's end, because by then I could not even get into the second team. Enter John Edrich, at that time a regular England opening batsman of legendary bravery and great effectiveness. He had obviously spotted my miserable efforts and took me aside one day to tell me, 'You can bowl fast, stick to your own style and work hard at that.' His words were a godsend. If a man who had battled away against the fastest in the world thought I was quick, who was I to disagree? I could not recall one delivery out of thousands I had sent down to Edrich in the nets which had disconcerted him in the slightest, but I must have had something. His confidence in me was an enormous boost and two years later he was again to play a crucial part in my career when he persuaded Ray Illingworth to fly me out to Australia as a replacement for the injured Alan Ward, a trip that started my long association with the England team.

I have recounted the Arthur McIntyre story with no animosity at all towards my genial former coach. Arthur taught me many things about self-discipline, mental strength and positive attitude and he was a constructive influence in general on my development. But, in common with many coaches in first-class cricket, he did not fully appreciate the make-up of a fast bowler. He failed to

The moment when all the sweat, the heartache and the training seems worthwhile. Norman Cowans
runs off the pitch after winning the Melbourne Test of 1982 with an inspired spell of controlled fast
bowling. Norman proved how meteoric a rise a fast bowler can enjoy: within a handful of years he had
graduated from school cricket to Test cricket without even spending a full season in the county game.
No other sphere of cricket endeavour provides such scope for dramatic development as fast bowling
– yet, as Norman soon found out, it is not enough simply to bowl fast. If Dennis Lillee admits he is still
learning, even though he is the leading Test wicket-taker, then we all must keep our minds open.
The fast bowler who thinks he knows it all will never be a force in county cricket, never mind for
his country.

realize that the young Willis model was never going to be a classical one, but it
could still be highly effective due to one priceless asset – the ability to bowl fast.
It took the common sense and experience of John Edrich to grasp that in the nick
of time for the sake of my career. How many other young English quick bowlers
have had my luck?

The ambitious youngster should also think hard about equipment, making
sure he feels as comfortable as he can while trying to bowl fast and accurately. It
follows that someone dedicated in his training and technical application should
be thorough about his boots, flannels and shirts. In club cricket, the fast bowler is
usually content with a pair of flannels that will not split as he runs in, a white shirt
of any fabric and a serviceable pair of boots. Once he starts playing the game for
a living he has to be less slapdash, particularly about his footwear. As with fast-
bowling actions, no two pairs of feet are the same and the result is that first-class
cricketers have their boots tailor-made for fast bowling. The feet are valuable

and must be looked after, so get the best quality available and make sure they suit your feet perfectly; they will be your greatest ally during a long, hot day in the field. Fast bowlers need a strong ankle-support to withstand jarring and I would also recommend a heel pad inside the boot to cope with the pounding action needed to bowl fast. A bruised heel is very painful indeed and your bowling suffers as a result. After a time, you find you cannot bang your foot down hard on the pitch at the moment of delivery, so your pace declines. If you cannot get a heel pad, do the next best thing and use foam rubber. Supplement that with a couple of pairs of socks as a further cushion – wool is best for a bowler because it absorbs moisture better and retains the softness in the sock that keeps feet healthy. Woollen socks also keep your feet cool in hot, sticky conditions. For shirt and trousers, flannel is as good as anything for a fast bowler – it copes best of all with perspiration and stops the shirt clinging uncomfortably to the body when bowling. A fast bowler needs plenty of room in both shirt and trousers to allow him scope to stretch himself, particularly in the groin, thigh and chest regions.

Always take at least one sweater out on to the field and put it on after bowling an over, no matter how hot the day. As perspiration dries off you can get a chill on the back which leads to stiffness and a decline in effectiveness. On a cold day, bring two sweaters out on to the field and always ensure there is another one handy in your bag in the dressing-room if you are feeling cold and stiff after a long bowl. I would also wear a vest to avoid back chills. Some fast bowlers even wear back flannels – a strip of cloth strapped around the midriff at the base of the spine – and I see nothing wrong in this if it wards off cold and stiffness. A captain wants his fast bowler to be at the peak of his performance whenever he throws him the ball and precautions taken to achieve that end should not be dismissed.

It really is a strain for the young quickie as he tries to cross the vast chasm between club and first-class cricket. Kind yet firm coaching, specialist advice, attention to detail, slices of luck, a positive attitude towards learning – all these must be grafted on to his natural talent. Above all, there is no excuse for not getting fit for the task in hand; lack of stamina is understandable in club players who may be desk-bound all week and play solely for fun in any event, but the professional has to possess 'a second wind', that extra burst of energy which takes wickets and inspires his side. The young county fast bowler should realize early on that he needs to be fitter than anyone else in the team, that the physical demands on him are greater than those faced by batsmen. Consequently, his training must be different and more exhaustive. If he gets stuck into organized, demanding training as soon as he joins the staff, he will endure an arduous month or so – but at least he will have started on the right foot, realizing that dedication is essential.

As he gets older and the strain of bowling fast becomes greater, his long-term training programme will prove invaluable. If he is lucky enough to play for England, he will find his stamina tested even more demandingly, particularly in the heat and tension of an overseas tour. The rewards for such dedication are now extremely attractive, but a great deal of sweat has to be shed in the process.

Within a few years, the lucky young fast bowler will have jumped from playing for his school to representing his country. At the age of 15, he might never have used a new ball in a match; five years later, he might be given one just after taking off his England sweater at the start of his first bowling stint in Test cricket. Between those years will be a catalogue of blood, sweat and tears and the achievement will be to his credit, irrespective of the amount of guidance from others. Success in fast bowling is very much in the hands of the individual.